PHILADELPHIA
A RAILROAD
HISTORY

EDWARD W. DUFFY

Camino Books, Inc.
Philadelphia

Copyright © 2013 by Edward W. Duffy
All rights reserved

No part of this book may be reproduced in any form or by any electronic or mechanical means including information storage and retrieval systems without permission in writing from the publisher, except by a reviewer who may quote brief passages in a review.

Manufactured in the United States of America

2 3 4 5   19 18 17 16

Library of Congress Cataloging-in-Publication Data

Duffy, Edward W., 1947–
  Philadelphia: a railroad history / Edward W. Duffy.
      p. cm.
  Includes bibliographical references and index.
  ISBN 978-1-933822-69-3 (alk. paper)
  1. Railroads—Pennsylvania—Philadelphia—History.
  2. Philadelphia (Pa.)—Buildings, structures, etc. I. Title.
  TF25.P5D84 2012
  385.09748'11—dc23   2012019841

Cover and interior design: Jerilyn Bockorick

The Chapter 6 opening showing the Pennsylvania Railroad GG–1 electric locomotive appears courtesy of the Philadelphia City Planning Commission from their August 1959 report, *Philadelphia Railroads*, which featured this depiction on the front cover.

The map on the back cover showing regional rail ownership and operation was provided courtesy of SEPTA.

This book is available at a special discount on bulk purchases for promotional, business, and educational use.

Publisher
Camino Books, Inc
P.O. Box 59026
Philadelphia, PA 19102
www.caminobooks.com

"To know one place well is to know all places better."

—Eudora Welty

CONTENTS

ACKNOWLEDGMENTS

This book would not have been possible without the help of many friends who encouraged my interest in the history of Philadelphia and its railroads. I would especially like to thank John C. Nolan, Steve Bartlett, Ray Scheinfeld and Ed Zelinski, who shared with me many of the books that I referenced in its writing, and Joe Aylmer and Peg McLaughlin, who provided me with their families' oral histories "working on the railroad." Sadly, Fred Winkler of the Winchester and Western Railroad, who provided me with decades of resources, advice and encouragement, passed away during its writing. This book is dedicated to Fred.

I am indebted to the help of the staff of many Philadelphia area institutions who lent images or provided other valuable assistance: Jacqueline Shirley, Amanda Davis and Tom Dalfo of the Philadelphia Industrial Development Corporation; Nicole Joniec of the Library Company of Philadelphia; Hillary Kativa of the Historical Society of Pennsylvania; Chris Baer of the Hagley Museum; Alex Bartlett of the Germantown Historical Society of Philadelphia; Aurora Deschauteurs of the Free Library of Philadelphia; Megan Good of the Independence Seaport Museum, Philadelphia; Elizabeth Laurent of Girard College; Cristine McCollum of the Federal Reserve Bank of Philadelphia; and Nicholas Zmijewski of the Railroad Museum of Pennsylvania.

I must thank Bill Goetz of CSX and Harry Garforth of SEPTA for their expertise and time fact-checking key chapters, and SEPTA's Byron Comati and Andy Ferry for their help with mapping.

I want especially to thank John C. Van Horne, Edwin Wolf 2nd Director of the Library Company of Philadelphia, for his guidance in finding a publisher; without his advice this book would never have been printed. It has been an absolute delight working with Camino Books Publisher Ed Jutkowitz and Senior Editor Brad Fisher.

I thank my daughters Leigh, for her photography, and Fionna, for her IT guidance, and my wife Sue, my source of inspiration and constant encouragement.

INTRODUCTION

everal years ago, a meeting was convened in Philadelphia to discuss conflicting demands on the use of the city's Schuylkill riverfront in the downtown area known locally as Center City. The conflict pitted the CSX Railroad, a major freight hauler whose main line from Jacksonville to Montreal runs along the Schuylkill River through Center City, against a coalition of civic groups advocating for increased recreational use of the riverfront, notably the extension of Schuylkill River Park as a bike and jogging path in very close quarters with the freight tracks, and for the addition of at-grade track crossings to connect the path to adjacent gentrifying neighborhoods.

Somewhat unusual for an American city, Philadelphia's downtown boasts a large and growing residential population, moving not only into the city's renowned row house neighborhoods, but increasingly into lofts created out of the old, multistory industrial buildings that CSX's predecessor, the Baltimore and Ohio Railroad, once served along the Schuylkill River. Indeed, it is not hard to find these loft buildings with abandoned rail sidings leading to them.

CSX's position on shared access of the Schuylkill riverfront was described by Bill Goetz, their regional public affairs officer, who began by observing that no one in his right mind would design a railroad system resembling what now exists. He noted that today's rail network is CSX's inheritance, for better or worse, from its predecessors who created it as long as 150 years ago, when the needs of transportation and society were so very different, but that now it would be infeasible and cost-prohibitive to build a new rail system designed to current needs. For that reason, the CSX railroad track was here to stay, not to be relocated elsewhere, and at-grade rail crossings were something CSX wished to avoid at all cost. The forum ended amicably, with community groups getting some of their desired outcomes and CSX making its points on safety and liability and requiring the city to install at least one pedestrian overpass to Schuylkill River Park. Only time will tell whether anyone will regret the outcome.

Bill Goetz's comments on the origins of Philadelphia's rail system piqued my interest, because in an early period of my own career, I had been spent three years observing the reorganization of the old rail system of smaller regional bankrupt railroads into the Conrail era. Just out of the Army, I had gotten a job as assistant to the City Economist, working in the city's Commerce Department; several weeks later, Congress passed the Regional Rail Reorganization Act of 1973. Seven railroads in the Northeast and Mid-Atlantic regions were then in bankruptcy, system maintenance was being dangerously deferred, and service was erratic to the point where the profitable railroads of the West and South saw their business with the connecting eastern bankrupt lines withering as shippers deserted the railroad industry for alternative modes of transportation. The Regional Rail Reorganization Act, said to have been drafted by the legal department of the Union Pacific Railroad, was enacted with the intent to create a new network of Northeastern railroads. According to John W. Ingram, head of the Federal Railroad Administration, "What we want to do is take the best parts of those bad systems and drag a viable railroad, or railroads, out from under the wreckage of the bankrupts. The resulting system should be capable of providing service of adequate quality to meet user requirements, have the capacity to meet the needs of the region's commerce, improve efficiency in the use of resources, and should be financially viable."[1]

Soon after its passage, the City of Philadelphia was contacted by the rail reorganization planning bodies, the Federal Railroad Administration's U.S. Railway Association, the Interstate Commerce Commission's Rail Services Planning Office, and the Pennsylvania Department of Transportation, and shippers either individually or as members of the National Industrial Transportation League, and they were asked to comment on the evolving system plans. Mayor Frank Rizzo delegated this project to his Commerce Director, Harry Belinger, who assigned it to the City Economist, Jan Vagassky, and he named me his research assistant. Never having worked for a railroad, my exposure to this industry so far was negligible.

Having to start somewhere, I contacted the three railroads serving Philadelphia, the bankrupt Penn Central and Reading lines, both of whom were headquartered here, and the profitable Chessie System, successor to the B&O, and asked them to explain their business models and terminal operations to me. The railroads were more than happy to assist, as the staff that I met all shared a profound personal as well as professional interest in seeing the situation remedied. Dick Hasselman and Joe Folk of Penn Central provided me with internal studies of their systems and rail tours of their main and branch lines and yards, as did Dave Shaeffer of the Reading and Ed Drucker of the Chessie System. Philadelphia Industrial Development Corporation and the Delaware River Port Authority provided funds for the Commerce Department to hire a rail industry consultant, R.L. Banks & Associates, to provide us with an inventory of Philadelphia's freight rail facilities and advice on their significance to Philadelphia's port and industries, the physical condition of these facilities and their potential role in a reorganized system. If the Regional Rail Reorganization Act was written by the Union Pacific, then the city's testimony was largely developed by Philadelphia's port and industrial interests, its railroads and shippers.

At the end of the process, the federal government created the Consolidated Rail Corporation, or Conrail,[2] its second choice in the U.S. Railway Association's Final System Plan after the first choice, involving a greater, more competitive role for the

Chessie System, foundered on renegotiation of union work rules. The federal reorganization merged the most viable pieces of the bankrupts, excluded unprofitable branch lines from incorporation in the U.S. Railway Association's Final System Plan and then provided Conrail with extraordinary powers to abandon lines outside the regulatory framework of what was then the Interstate Commerce Commission. From its first day of operation, April 1, 1976, Conrail could, and did, abandon with gusto, and I had a front row seat to watch the dissolution of that old railroad era. This process accelerated with Congressional passage of the Staggers Act of 1980, effectively reducing the regulatory power of the ICC on the entire rail industry, as Conrail pressed for greater pricing flexibility with its freight customers and with more compensatory division of rates with its connecting rail carriers.

The detritus of the rail reorganization eventually settled out, Conrail became a profitable entity that ceded its predecessors' commuter passenger rail operations in the Philadelphia region to SEPTA and focused its considerable management talents on hauling freight long distances for large customers, in 1987 launching an initial public offering of its stock that rewarded the federal government with a $1.9 billion profit for its bailout. I went on to other projects in real estate development. Conrail's near monopoly over the rail freight business in its primarily east-west franchise area, where it competed only with the Delaware and Hudson Railroad, created problems for the big north-south carriers CSX and Norfolk Southern, who eventually seized Conrail in a hostile takeover and implemented another reorganization that resembled the Final System Plan's first-choice alternative, a truly more competitive rail environment in the Northeast and Midwest regions.

The rail reorganization process, extending from 1973 to 1976, allowed me to gain an insight into railroad issues, and occasionally I have been sought out to resolve, or at least attempt to resolve, some real estate matter, however obscure, left over from the railroads now long departed. This process has left me with knowledge of the rail system past and present, respect for those who created and operated it, and admiration for those who have made it function again, no matter how radical the surgery they had to perform in order to save it. There are plenty of stories of this industry's Philadelphia past, most mundane but some worth retelling, and that is what follows. An apology is offered in advance to anyone who is dismayed not to find his favorite story retold here.

In researching this book, I was impressed by the fact that the individuals who developed Philadelphia's railroads and related manufacturing industries were extraordinary in the scope of their interests and activities, both private and public. Stephen Girard set the gold standard. One of the three wealthiest men of his era, he not only left his estate for public benefactions in Philadelphia in 1831, but in the 1793 yellow fever epidemic, he was tireless in relieving the afflicted both by his generosity and his personal care of sick Philadelphians at the risk of his own health. Samuel V. Merrick, a founder and first president of the Pennsylvania Railroad, cofounded the Franklin Institute at age 23 in 1824. George Roberts, a PRR president, led the effort to relocate, deepen and widen the Port of Philadelphia's shipping channel and to improve the port's main thoroughfare, Delaware Avenue. John Towne, founder of the North Penn Railroad, endowed the University of Pennsylvania's engineering school. William Sellers, a director of the Reading Railroad, was president of Midvale Steel Company and the Franklin Institute as well as his own machine tool company in Bush Hill, and he led the city's planning of the 1876 Centennial. Sellers was responsible for its emphasis on technological advancement as displayed in Machinery Hall, his signature contribution to the exposition. In 1903, Baldwin Locomotive Company president Samuel Vauclain expanded Fairmount Park's Japanese Garden, first created as a Centennial exhibit. Business leaders of that era had in common a love for their city and for the advancement of their industries. They were members of the American Philosophical Society, forerunner of the U.S. Patent Office, and the Franklin Institute, both 19th-century incubators of American technological development. Philadelphia became known as the "Workshop of the World" because of their actions. Today, Philadelphians enjoy the results of their public spirit. The city is graced with their professional accomplishments, such as Reading Terminal and 30th Street Station, and they have left us hidden gems awaiting our discovery. Even the scoundrels of the era, such as Franklin B. Gowen, fascinate with the gargantuan extent of their hubris and sculduggery.

One explanatory note is necessary. The geographic definition of the City of Philadelphia changed in 1854, when the city and county governments were consolidated. Prior to January 31, 1854, the "city" was defined as extending for two miles between the Delaware and Schuylkill Rivers, and one mile from Vine Street on the north to South Street. Various townships existed throughout the rest of Philadelphia County before 1854 (for example, Northern Liberties and Penn Township, and Southwark Township), but after consolidation their functions were assumed by the City of Philadelphia, which was charged with governing the entire 129.4 square-mile county, as it does today.

References

1. Northeastern Railroad Investigation, Review of the Secretary of Transportation's Rail Service Report, Ex Parte 293 (Sub. No. 1), ICC. Statement made on behalf of Reading Company, Debtor, by Andrew L. Lewis, Jr., Trustee, March 4, 1974; quotation of FRA administrator John W. Ingram.
2. Dale W. Woodland, *The Reading in the Conrail Era*, Vol. I (Telford, PA: Silver Brook Junction Publishing Company, 1998), gives a description of Conrail's creation and public stock offering.

PHILADELPHIA
A RAILROAD
HISTORY

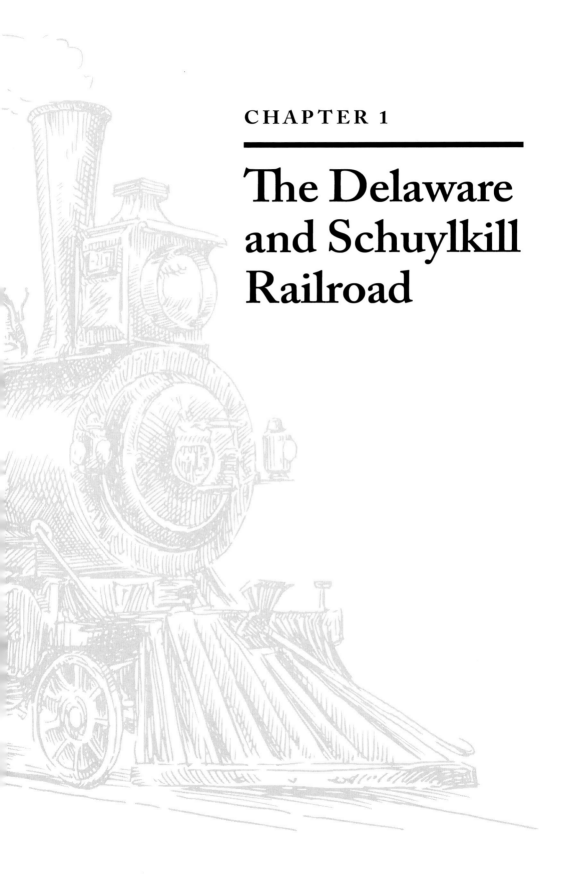

CHAPTER 1

The Delaware and Schuylkill Railroad

riving north from Center City Philadelphia on Broad Street, after crossing the Vine Street Expressway and Callowhill Street, one sees an old railroad dining car on the right, incongruously parked by the sidewalk. How did it get here, and why? The answer lies in the story of what most recently has been known as the Willow and Noble Street Branch of the Reading Railroad, of which this dining car is one of only a few traces. Before railroads there were canals, and the Delaware and Schuylkill Railroad incorporates the stories of both, so this chapter will begin with an account of its earlier life as a canal.

During his lifetime and especially during his presidency, George Washington was a forceful advocate for construction of inland waterways to connect the various rivers of the settled portions of the country as a means of developing the new nation's resources. While Washington is remembered as one of our greatest political and military leaders, he thought of himself primarily as a competent, experienced architect, engineer and surveyor—that is, a "Mason." Washington conducted voluminous correspondence offering his guidance regarding engineering projects such as construction of Philadelphia's Fort Mifflin, even during the most trying moments of the Revolutionary War, and he was universally respected for his engineering expertise. Among the prominent people that Washington convinced of the need for waterways was the Philadelphian Robert Morris (1734–1806), patriot and Revolutionary War financier. Canals were used extensively in Europe long before the American Revolution, and so it was natural that Washington's canal idea would catch on as soon as independence had been achieved and growing population and commerce required better transportation facilities.

In January 1791, a group of businessmen met to discuss various possible ideas for transportation improvements in the Philadelphia area, and from this meeting the Society for the Improvement of Roads and Inland Navigation was formed; Robert Morris was elected its president. Initially, the Society focused its energies on turnpike development, but in 1792, members of the Society formed the Delaware and Schuylkill Canal Navigation Company to construct a canal from the east bank of the Schuylkill River eastward across what was then the northern boundary of the city until the Delaware River was reached. Another canal segment was proposed along the Schuylkill River to link it with Reading by way of Norristown and with points north and west of Reading, eventually reaching the Susquehanna River in the vicinity of Columbia, Pennsylvania.

Philadelphia, in the 1790s the nation's capital and its largest city and seaport, was growing rapidly, having become the second largest English-speaking city in the world. As a result of this growth, it encountered three common problems of urbanization: mysterious epidemics, uncontrollable fires and scarcity of fuel. Development of a canal, it was hoped, could address these problems by creating a fresh, large and reliable source of water for consumption and firefighting, and by providing bituminous coal as an alternative to firewood.

The involvement of Robert Morris was fortuitous in that he owned a large estate over which he offered to create the canal's right-of-way. Now known as Lemon Hill, "The Hills" was located just north of the city in an area that had seen very little development as it had been retained by the Penn family for their own estate, "Springettsbury," which originally extended the entire distance from the Schuylkill to the Delaware. The Penns had given a portion of Springettsbury (named for William Penn's first wife, Gulielma Maria Springett) to Andrew Hamilton in 1735 in payment for his legal services, and Hamilton developed his own estate, Bush Hill, adjacent to The Hills.

Andrew Hamilton (1676–1741) is known as the original "Philadelphia lawyer" for his successful defense of John Peter Zenger, a German-born printer who was charged with libel by the colonial governor of New York because he had published a report of the governor's interference in the processes of the courts. Hamilton took the irrefutable position that if Zenger's report were truthful, then libel could not result. Hamilton went on to other successes. He is credited with the design of Independence Hall, and with the financial help of his son-in-law, Pennsylvania Supreme Court Justice William Allen, he carried out its construction, beginning in 1732,[14] but he is best remembered for Zenger's acquittal in 1735. Today's Hamilton Street, which parallels the City Branch, is named for him.

Bush Hill (Watercolor by David J. Kennedy, courtesy of The Historical Society of Pennsylvania).

Morris purchased Bush Hill and conveyed a right-of-way across it to the Delaware and Schuylkill Canal Navigation Company. Construction began well enough with the completion of the segment from Norristown to Philadelphia's Pennsylvania Avenue at Fairmount, but then the project faltered. It was partially dug as far east as Broad Street, following the contours of the land, which was drained by a meandering, willow-lined creek known as Pegg's Run or Cohocksink, meaning "pinelands" in the native Lenape language. The canal began again at 11th Street and stopped near 8th. Morris ran into financial difficulties, which led to his incarceration in Philadelphia's debtors' prison from February 1798 until August 1801. The Hills was sold at bankruptcy auction to Henry Pratt, who built the current Lemon Hill mansion. By 1802, canal construction work had ceased entirely on the project segment crossing Philadelphia, but the Schuylkill Canal portion was completed from Port Carbon and Reading to Fairmount (in the vicinity of Lemon Hill) in 1826 when shipments began.

There remained the unanswered questions of protecting and improving the city's water supply and developing coal as a fuel alternative. In the 1790s, Philadelphia experienced annual summer yellow fever epidemics, which many erroneously attributed to foul drinking water whose source was polluted groundwater, although the actual cause was germs carried by mosquitoes breeding in rain barrels and stagnant pools of water. The disease may have been brought to Philadelphia in the bloodstreams of refugees fleeing the turmoil engulfing Haiti as its slaves fought for the goals of liberty, equality and fraternity that they believed were promised by the French Revolution. Between August and November 1791, 4,002 deaths from yellow fever were recorded; for those same months in 1793, the death toll was 4,044, including 625 members of the congregation of St. Michael's Lutheran Church; for 1797, it was 1,292; for 1798, it was 3,637, these deaths occurring in an era when the city's population was estimated to be 41,200, and the county's total population was about 61,000.[6] The canal company's charter had provided for the sale of potable water to the city, but the city opted for an alternative, creating a basin in the Schuylkill River off Chestnut Street. From there, beginning on January 21, 1801, water was pumped by stationary steam engine to a 16,000-gallon water tower at Centre Square, the current location of Philadelphia's City Hall. The city quickly outgrew this system, and in 1811, City Council approved chief engineer Frederick Graff's plan to move the plant upstream to Fairmount, creating Philadelphia's beautiful waterworks. As a result, a possible revenue source was lost to the canal company. Initially powered by a wood-burning stationary steam engine, it was soon converted to a water mill. Philadelphia's Fairmount Water Works was not only one of America's first water treatment plants, it was one of its first tourist attractions.[3]

The yellow fever epidemics required selfless and heroic measures. Physicians believed that there was a need to remove the ill, as a possible source of contagion, to a place that was isolated but not remote. The former Penn estate lands were ideal,

Bush Hill in 1848 (Illustration by David J. Kennedy, courtesy of The Historical Society of Pennsylvania).

with Morris' Bush Hill mansion recently vacated by Vice President John Adams, who had left the city. Bush Hill was temporarily converted to a hospital under the administration of Stephen Girard (1750–1831). Girard, a native of Bordeaux, France, had settled in Philadelphia in 1769 as a shipmaster and merchant engaging in the West Indian and American coastal trade. After the Revolutionary War, his business rapidly increased. True to his motto that "The love of labor is my highest ambition," Girard's bravery, kindness and tireless work during the epidemic should be remembered as an even greater legacy than the immense wealth that he accumulated and willed to Girard College and to the City of Philadelphia.[3] Occasionally, he must have looked up from his work ministering to the needs of the ill and dying to gaze out the window and marvel at the beauty of the lands of the Bush Hill estate surrounding this pestilence-filled house.

Thus began an era in which the relatively open and undeveloped Bush Hill vicinity west of Broad Street was identified as the ideal location for large public institutions, such as Eastern State Penitentiary; Preston Retreat, one of America's first maternity hospitals; and Girard College, endowed by Girard for orphan boys. This was in contrast to the area nearer the Delaware River east of Broad Street. Under Thomas Penn, son of William and his second wife Hannah Callowhill Penn and his son John, this area developed quite rapidly and with much greater density than Bush Hill. Known then and now as Northern Liberties, this eastern section was the sixth largest American town in 1800.[6]

During this time, work continued on the Schuylkill Canal, and a potential business opportunity of bonanza proportions now appeared within its investors' reach. Elsewhere in the United States, consumers were beginning to use bituminous or "English" coal in place of firewood. Some of this fuel began appearing in Philadelphia, but it was expensive because there were no nearby sources. Indeed, in the 1790s, other canal plans had been floated, linking the Delaware, Schuylkill and Susquehanna Rivers, for the purpose of accessing bituminous coalfields.

There was plenty of locally available coal, but it was anthracite or hard coal; at the time no one knew quite how to ignite it. A Philadelphia iron foundry, Josiah White's Fairmount Nail and Iron Works, was importing Virginia bituminous coal for its processes, but White was aware of the presence of the anthracite variety at the head of the Schuylkill, and in 1812, he began experimenting with it. White had brought some of the anthracite coal down in wagons at a cost of a dollar per bushel or $28 per ton, and had spent what seemed to him a small fortune, but he could not succeed in making it burn. His millworkers became exasperated trying to ignite it, and the experiment was about to be abandoned when late one afternoon, after having tried once more without success, they gave up, threw a large quantity of "black stones" into the furnace, shut the doors and went home. One worker had left his jacket in the mill and on returning for it, he discovered a tremendous fire in the

Stephen Girard (Courtesy of Girard College).

furnace, its doors red with heat. White was notified and immediately ordered three separate heats of iron with that one fire. This was the first practical use of anthracite, based on the discovery that all that was needed to ignite it was time.[6] On making this discovery, Josiah White (1781–1850) began experiments to invent various grates to make anthracite available for domestic use. For the canal company, there now existed a product ideal for conveyance by water to the Philadelphia market. The plentiful anthracite nearby in Schuylkill County produced much greater heat than either firewood or bituminous coal, and unlike these other fuels, it generated much less smoke and sparks, making it nearly perfect for heating homes.

Josiah White packed his carpetbag and headed for the wilderness camp of Mauch Chunk ("bear mountain" in Lenape) on the banks of the Lehigh River in Pennsylvania's Pocono Mountains, where he bought his supplier's mine and leased the rights to mine another 20,000 acres. But before White could mine successfully, he would first have to overcome a logistics conundrum, and he approached this with the enthusiasm, creativity and energy that marked all of the projects that he undertook throughout his life. First, White successfully petitioned the state legislature for the right to construct a canal on the Lehigh, running from Mauch Chunk (now Jim Thorpe) to Easton, where his canal would join the existing state-constructed Delaware Canal leading to Philadelphia. Easton's sister city of Phillipsburg, on the New Jersey side of the Delaware, was linked to Newark and New York by the Morris Canal. White created a towing cable crossing of the Delaware so that his canal boats could pass onto the Morris Canal and access the New York market.[2]

In the times when Josiah White was developing his anthracite business, railroads had yet to be invented, and two decades would pass before a steam locomotive appeared in Philadelphia. White was forced to rely on water and animal power, but his solutions were original. He built a nine-mile-long road from the mine at Summit Hill to the Lehigh Canal, "laid out with instruments scientifically, on the principle of never rising"—that is, downhill all the way for the loaded car, the first instance of this design being employed in the United States. Then, to improve the road's all-weather usefulness, he laid on wooden rails, creating a "railed road." Gravity took the cars down to the canal, but White had to get the emptied cars back up to the mine using mule power, and that raised the question of transporting the mules back down. His logistical solution was simple. A separate train consisting of seven wagons each holding four mules was sent downhill, a boy in each car feeding them hay along the ride to allay their motion sickness. This was the first railroad dining car, as White was often fond of saying.

Josiah White's first coal shipment to Philadelphia, 365 tons in 1820, comprised over 80 percent of all anthracite mined that year in Pennsylvania. Within five years, statewide tonnage had risen to 43,000. White, however, did not confine his energy to his coalmining operation; in 1815, he had led a successful effort to reorganize the canal-building project along the Schuylkill, despite opposition over the loss of shad fishing, extending it beyond Stoney Creek in Norristown to Reading and Port Carbon, a distance of 108 miles from the Fairmount dam. A so-called slack water system, the canal consisted of 58 miles of canals, 50 miles of pools, 129 locks, 34 dams, one tunnel 385 feet long and a rise of 610 feet when opened for its entire distance in 1826.

The most successful canal of this era, indeed in American history, was New York's Erie Canal linking Albany with Buffalo, the Hudson River with the Great Lakes, begun on July 4, 1818 and completed in 1825 over the so-called water level route—a distance of 362 miles, forever transforming commerce in the Northeast and Mid-Atlantic regions as New York City assumed leadership in trade and population over Philadelphia.

Alarmed Philadelphians petitioned the Pennsylvania legislature in 1828 to create a competing route from Philadelphia to the American interior at Pittsburgh, but the terrain across Pennsylvania was far more daunting than what New York had to overcome. When completed, the state-funded, 394-mile project known as the Main Line of Public Works consisted of an 82-mile-long railroad from Philadelphia via Lancaster to Columbia on the Susquehanna River, a 171-mile-long canal from Columbia to Hollidaysburg, the 37-mile-long Allegheny Portage Railroad over the mountains to Johnstown, and a 104-mile canal to Pittsburgh. This entire system was completed in 1834, nine years after the Erie Canal had opened for business, a critical period during which the American railroad industry had been created. Already the New York and Erie Railroad had begun construction of a rail line paralleling the Erie Canal. The end of the canal era was in sight.[1]

The Commonwealth of Pennsylvania's rail line to the Susquehanna, known as the Philadelphia and Columbia Railroad, ended on the west bank of the Schuylkill River, at the foot of Belmont Plateau in today's Fairmount Park. East of the Schuylkill, the Pennsylvania Canal Commission constructed a railroad track in the bed of Robert Morris' abandoned canal, now owned by the Union Canal Company, as far east as Broad Street to a terminal at Vine Street. The Schuylkill River was crossed with the covered, seven-span "Columbia Bridge" having double tracks and a cartway. The Philadelphia train outbound for Columbia climbed the Belmont Plateau by means of an inclined plane a half-mile long with a seven percent grade, employing a stationary steam engine at its crest turning a drum to tow the train by cable up the hill. A westbound passenger boarded a railroad passenger car at Broad and Vine at 8:00 a.m. and arrived in Pittsburgh on the afternoon of the fourth day, changing conveyances four times. As annoying and time-consuming as this trip must have been, the passenger counted himself fortunate on completing it, as service ceased entirely during winter months when the canals were frozen or when they were damaged by heavy rains or interrupted by low water during the summer droughts. The passenger's annoyance would immediately change to horror if halfway

Belmont inclined plane of the Commonwealth of Pennsylvania's Main Line of Public Works, 1840 (Lithograph by J.T. Brown). This view is eastward from Belmont Mansion toward the Schuylkill River, crossed by covered bridge. The right-of-way of the inclined plane can still be traced in Belmont Mansion's vicinity (Courtesy of The Library Company of Philadelphia).

up the Belmont plane, the train detached from the towing cable. None of these obstacles would stop service on the New York and Erie Railroad.

A traveler of 1836 described her ride up the Belmont Plateau: "At the foot of the inclined plane the horses were loosed from the cars, several of which were tied to an endless rope, moved by a steam engine placed on the top of the plane, and presently began to mount the acclivity with the speed of five miles per hour. No accident occurred, notwithstanding old Mrs. Redridinghood had frightened one of our company out of the car by a direful tale of broken ropes and necks and legs and arms. When the cars had all arrived at the top of the plane, some 12 or 14 were strung together like beads, and fastened to the latter end of a steam tug, which was already wheezing, puffing and smoking, as if anxious to be off." Such was the start of the Philadelphia railroad traveler's journey to the West.[10]

The level of dissatisfaction with the service, or often the lack thereof, on the Main Line of Public Works drew calls for creating a direct route from Philadelphia to Pittsburgh, but the real impetus was the imminent arrival in Pittsburgh of the

Baltimore and Ohio Railroad, then extending its track northwestward from Baltimore through Harper's Ferry. Pittsburgh, in the 1840s, the third largest city west of the Allegheny Mountains after New Orleans and Cincinnati, was quite a prize for railroads as it had sizable industries of its own, particularly iron and glass manufacturing. If the B&O could reach Pittsburgh, much valuable traffic would be lost to the Public Works, and Philadelphia would forfeit the trade of the western end of Pennsylvania to Baltimore. A "Railroad Convention" was held in Harrisburg in January 1846 to argue whether a bill supporting the B&O or one authorizing creation of a Pennsylvania Railroad should be adopted. The B&O proposal met defeat by only a single vote, and the Pennsylvania Railroad Company, largely a Philadelphia creation, was chartered on April 13, 1846.

The PRR's Philadelphia organizers included Thomas P. Cope, principal of the Cope Line, whose four ships engaged in the Liverpool trade from the Cope pier at the foot of Walnut Street; David S. Brown, a prominent merchant in Philadelphia and Gloucester; Samuel V. Merrick, who became the PRR's first president, serving from 1846 until 1849; Steven Colwell, an iron manufacturer; and James Magee, whose ship, the *Commerce*, traded between Philadelphia and New Orleans. A life member of the American Philosophical Society, Samuel Merrick (1801–1870) at the age of 23 cofounded the Franklin Institute and served as its president from 1842 until 1854. His businesses included the Southwark Iron Foundry and Merrick & Sons machine works, builders of stationary, fire and ship steam engines and the original Philadelphia Gas Works.

While Philadelphia's attempts to remain competitive for interior markets were disappointing, the city's full embrace of the Industrial Revolution brought it rapid and unforeseen prosperity, much of it as a result of the Schuylkill Canal. On Tuesday, December 5, 1826, the first steamboat on the canal reached Reading from Philadelphia, attaining four miles per hour in the canals and eight miles per hour in the dam pools. In 1827, the Union Canal connecting the Schuylkill with the Susquehanna River was completed, and the Schuylkill Canal collected 1,000 tons of freight from that source during its first year of operation. The Schuylkill Canal's owner, Schuylkill Navigation Company, enjoyed its greatest prosperity from 1835 to 1841, and the canal's locks were enlarged in 1846 to accommodate 160-ton coal barges drawing five feet of water. About 600 canal boats regularly engaged in this coal traffic, many of them operating through to New York and points on Long Island Sound as far as New London, Connecticut.[2]

By 1859, the Schuylkill Canal achieved its maximum traffic of 1.7 million tons, of which almost 1.4 million were anthracite. By this time, the canal company also owned its own fleet of yellow railroad freight cars, which were actively used by the many small railroads springing up in the Schuylkill County coal country. This acted as a catalyst for the canal company and the largest of the Schuylkill County railroads, the Philadelphia and Reading, to coordinate their operations to better service their mutual coal trade.[7]

The year 1869 was disastrous for the Schuylkill Navigation Company. First there was a bitter, six-week miners' strike in May and June that almost completely stopped coal shipments. This was followed by an August drought of such severity that the city was forced to draw so much water from the Schuylkill River that navigation became impossible. Then, on October 4th, came the greatest flood ever seen on the Schuylkill, destroying the company physically and financially. In 1870, control of the company was surrendered to the Philadelphia and Reading Railroad.

Meanwhile, development of railroads in Philadelphia had already begun, with the first charter being issued to the Delaware and Schuylkill Railroad, incorporated in April 1829, and completed and opened on April 23, 1834 by the Pennsylvania Canal Commission. This horse-drawn railroad followed the right-of-way of Robert Morris' failed canal along Pegg's Run west through Bush Hill to the Schuylkill River at Peter's Island, across from the Philadelphia terminus of the Commonwealth of Pennsylvania's Philadelphia and Columbia Railroad, which had opened three weeks earlier. A bridge connected the two lines there. The canal commission's passenger station was located at Broad and Vine Streets, and the Delaware and Schuylkill's combined railroad depot and hotel was located at the northwest corner of Third and Willow Streets. The portion of the line between the Delaware River and Broad Street was known as the Northern Liberties and Penn Township Railroad, or simply as the Willow Street Line.[7]

As noted earlier, the Pennsylvania Railroad was chartered in April 1846 to acquire and upgrade the commonwealth's Main Line of Public Works from Philadelphia to Pittsburgh. Funds were raised through sale of stock to purchase the line, and the company was organized in 1847, with the purchase of the Main Line consummated in 1857 for $7,500,000. Early on, the PRR's management recognized that their new railroad's entry to Philadelphia via the Belmont inclined plane was unsatisfactory, and they constructed a new line 7.5 miles long from Ardmore to West Philadelphia, terminating at the Market Street Bridge over the Schuylkill, with operation beginning in October 1850. After this the Belmont inclined plane, the line of track from the Broad Street Station to the Schuylkill and the Columbia Bridge across the Schuylkill connecting them were sold at auction to the Philadelphia and Reading Railroad.[1]

The Philadelphia and Reading Railroad had its origins in the Blue Mountains northeast of Reading in 1826, with the original intention of constructing a canal there on the east branch of the Schuylkill River. It was soon determined that this branch, the "Little Schuylkill," was not capable of sustaining a navigable waterway, and the managers decided that building a railroad would be easier. The guiding force behind the company was a Reading doctor, Isaac Hiester, who had the good fortune to partner with a recent German immigrant, Dr. Friedrich List. List had worked as an associate of the British engineer George Stevenson, who built his first steam locomotive in 1814, and a greatly improved model in the following year. Stevenson was not the first to develop a locomotive. Inventions occurred in 1804 in

Map of Central Philadelphia, 1925 (From the author's collection).

Philadelphia, where Oliver Evans (1755–1819) drove about the city in his self-propelled amphibious dredge commissioned by the Philadelphia Health Department, and in London, where a locomotive was created by Richard Trevithick. List was an avid believer in the potential that steam locomotives possessed, and he shared his enthusiasm with Dr. Hiester, and also with Steven Girard, financier of the War of 1812 and by then America's wealthiest man. Girard became their third partner, underwriting their venture. The fourth partner in this enterprise was a young Virginia engineer, Moncure Robinson (1802–1891). Construction began on a right-of-way using metal-covered wooden rails and horsepower. It was not until two years later, in 1833, that two British engines arrived through the Port of Philadelphia for service on the line.

Not in any mood to rest on their accomplishments, the P&R Railroad petitioned the Commonwealth of Pennsylvania in April 1833 for a charter to extend its line down the entire length of the Schuylkill Navigation Company's canal to Fairmount in Philadelphia. One might have expected a strong negative response from the canal company, but it was less than anticipated, because in reality the two companies were managed by almost identical boards of directors and shared the same chief engineer, Moncure Robinson. Robinson surveyed the rail line to Belmont along the canal on the west bank of the Schuylkill and then connected it to the Delaware and Schuylkill Railroad at Fairmount. Robinson opened the P&R's Philadelphia passenger station in 1839 at the southeast corner of Broad and Cherry Streets. Its first ticket agent, David J. Kennedy (1816?–1898), was an artist whose watercolors are included in this book. Kennedy also was the agent at the second passenger station, located at Broad and Callowhill Streets, erected in 1861.[7]

Well before 1861, the area in the vicinity of Broad and Callowhill Streets, the site of Andrew Hamilton's Bush Hill estate, was taking on the character of one of America's first industrial centers. Philadelphia had developed industry soon after William Penn's arrival in 1682. Its location along the fall line separating the piedmont from the tidewater plain provided it with ample fast-flowing streams and creeks to harness water to power mills such as Willem Rittinghuysen's paper mill, the first in British North America when built in 1690. Thus it was natural for Philadelphia to harness the new technology of the steam engine to mill functions when it made its appearance on American shores. The steam engine's power allowed for construction of larger factories, and the open fields of Bush Hill beckoned the technicians and entrepreneurs laboring in nearby Philadelphia.[3]

The steam engine had been around, at least in theory, since the time of Hero of Alexandria, whose 120 B.C. treatise *Pneumatica* described a steam turbine and several forms of steam fountains and boilers, but its first practical application did not occur until 1650, when Edward Somerset constructed a steam engine to raise water from the moat to the top of the tower of Raglan Castle in Monmouthshire, in southwest England. The modern steam engine is attributed to Thomas Newcomen, who received a patent in 1705, and this engine was improved by James Watt, who added many accessories.[9] Its first successful application to transportation was made by John Fitch on the Schuylkill River at the foot of Market Street in 1785. The artist Rembrandt Peale provided an eyewitness account of this event:

> "In the Spring of 1785, hearing there was something curious to be seen at the floating bridge on the Schuylkill at Market Street, I eagerly ran to the spot, where I found a few persons collected and eagerly gazing at a shallop at anchor below the bridge with about twenty persons on board. On the deck was a small furnace, and machinery connected with a coupling crank, projecting over the stern to give motion to three or four paddles, resembling snow shovels, which

hung into the water. When all was ready, and the power of steam was made to act, by means of which I was then ignorant, knowing nothing of the piston except in the common pump, the paddles began to work, pressing against the water backward as they rose, and the boat, to my great delight, moved against the tide, without wind or hand . . . and proceeded slowly to its destination at Gray's Ferry. So far it must have been satisfactory to Mr. Fitch in this his first public experiment."[10]

Philadelphia in the 1790s was the center of American technological innovation, thanks in no small part to the presence of the United States Patent Office in the building housing the American Philosophical Society, which counted among its leaders Benjamin Franklin, David Rittenhouse and Thomas Jefferson. Founded in 1743 by Benjamin Franklin "for the promoting of Useful Knowledge in medicine, science, brewing and any improvement in the Power of Man over Matter," the Society provided like-minded technologists interested in metalworking and mechanical applications with a place to meet and discuss their latest theories and projects. By the 1820s, numerous small manufacturing shops had sprung up in Philadelphia, many within walking distance of the Society, located then and now near the southwest corner of 5th and Chestnut Streets, adjacent to Independence Hall. It is no exaggeration to say that the American Philosophical Society provided the incubator for the American Industrial Revolution, literally in the shadow of Andrew Hamilton's Independence Hall. One can imagine the excitement in the Society's assembly room, packed with young entrepreneurs, metalsmiths, and tool and die makers awaiting Oliver Evans to step to the podium and deliver his treatise on his application of the steam engine to autolocomotion, or for Benjamin Latrobe to present his plans to build the steam-powered Schuylkill River waterworks at Centre Square.[4]

No doubt one of those attendees would have been a young jeweler, Matthias Baldwin (1795–1866), who upon completing his apprenticeship, joined the Philadelphia firm of Fletcher & Gardener, Silversmiths, in 1817. Having mastered the basics of metalworking there, he expanded his interests, forming a partnership in 1824 to produce tools for other trades, including the textile industry. Moving to a larger shop in the center of Philadelphia, Baldwin created his own power source by building his own stationary steam engine in 1825, and he continued to employ this engine to power various Baldwin shops until finally donating it to the Smithsonian Institution.[8]

The success of this novel engine brought orders for more, so that by the late 1820s, Baldwin had come to be recognized as Philadelphia's go-to expert on this new technology. In 1829, the application of this type of engine to move a vehicle on a track composed of iron rails was proved feasible at the British Rainhill Trials when locomotives built by George Stephenson, Timothy Hackworth and John Ericsson

Matthias Baldwin (From the author's collection).

competed for a week in a series of rigorous tests won by Stephenson's aptly named *Rocket.* Philadelphians closely followed reports on the trials and eagerly awaited the appearance of steam locomotives on their own rail line, the Philadelphia and Columbia, then under construction.

A Philadelphia merchant, Franklin Peale, Rembrandt Peale's brother, commissioned Baldwin to build a model steam locomotive that ran on a circular track pulling two passenger carriages in Peale's Philadelphia Museum. Baldwin completed his creation without ever having seen another locomotive, and he followed it up with *Old Ironsides,* an industrial-strength, five-ton locomotive that he sold to the Philadelphia, Germantown and Norristown Railroad in 1832. After a payment dispute with the buyer, Baldwin vowed never to produce another locomotive, but the success of *Old Ironsides* brought a flood of new orders to his factory at 4th and Walnut Streets, which he quickly outgrew when given the commission to create seven engines for the Philadelphia and Columbia Railroad in 1834. Baldwin now felt confident enough in his enterprise to build a substantial factory, completed in 1836, and he chose a location in Bush Hill fronting on Broad and Hamilton Streets. The presence of the Delaware and Schuylkill Railroad there was already recognized as ideal for a factory catering to the rail industry, and in short order Bush Hill became the home not only of Baldwin, but also of a cluster of metalworking, rail-oriented manufacturers and innovators. These included Baldwin's competitor William Norris & Son, Bush Hill Iron Works, William Sellers' iron foundry and machine shop, Stanley G. Flagg Malleable Iron Works, Bement & Dougherty machine builders, and Hoopes & Townsend nut and bolt manufacturers. Also nearby were Baldwin's partner Asa Whitney (1791–1874), the former New York State canal commissioner, who became the largest manufacturer of railroad wheels in the United States and president of the P&R (1860–61); John Evans, who supplied Baldwin with springs for his locomotives; as well as assorted carpet, cotton and woolen mills, breweries, granaries, and ice and coal distributors. Bush Hill had evolved into Philadelphia's first and arguably most successful industrial park.

These entrepreneurs had their roots in the idea-sharing environment of the American Philosophical Society and the Franklin Institute, established in 1824 three blocks away on South 7th Street, and they found time in their schedules to continue sponsoring and advocating technological and civic advancement. Matthias Baldwin served on the boards of the Franklin Institute and the Philadelphia County Prison, spoke out as an abolitionist, and assisted in the creation of the Civil War Sanitary Commission. His partner Samuel Vauclain purchased the 1904 St. Louis World's Fair exhibit known as the Japanese Pagoda, or Nio-mon, and had it transported to Philadelphia and reassembled at the site of the 1876 Centennial Exhibition's Japanese Garden in Fairmount Park. William Sellers (1824–1905), whose Midvale Steel Works supplied nearly all the material (with the exception of the steel cables) for the Brooklyn Bridge, is considered to be one of the greatest mechanical engineers of his era. He was a member of the American Philosophical

Aerial view of Baldwin Locomotive Works (Courtesy of the Print and Picture Collection, Free Library of Philadelphia).

Society and the Academy of Natural Sciences, president of the Franklin Institute (1864–67), a manager of the P&R Railroad (1860–65), a member of the board of trustees of the University of Pennsylvania and a founder of Philadelphia's Union League.[2] Sellers resided at 1819 Vine Street, a short walk from his machine shop. It was largely through his influence that the Centennial Exhibition's Machinery Hall focused the world's attention on technological innovation. William Bement (1817–1897), residing at 1814 Spring Garden Street, was chairman of the Franklin Institute and served on the board of the Pennsylvania Academy of the Fine Arts from 1874 until his death. Engineers and inventors achieved celebrity status in 19th-century Philadelphia as the public closely followed their discoveries and honored their accomplishments. A monument was erected to Frederick Graff, designer, builder and operator of the Fairmount Water Works; it was dedicated on June 1, 1848 and thought to be the first such honor bestowed on an engineer in the United States. In addition, a statue honoring Matthias Baldwin was erected at Centre Square.

Within a dozen years of his move to Bush Hill, Baldwin transformed his company into the leading locomotive builder in the United States, employing hundreds of workers and making Bush Hill into one of America's busiest industrial zones, extending from Spring Garden Street south to Callowhill Street, and from 22nd Street to 13th Street, encompassing over 50 acres. The area to its north soon

Street-level view of Baldwin Locomotive Works, Broad Street (Courtesy of PhillyHistory.org, a project of the Philadelphia Department of Records).

filled with the elegant three- and four-story row homes of the business managers along Spring Garden Street and the mansions of the owners along Vine, Green and Mount Vernon Streets. Across from Baldwin's headquarters at Broad and Spring Garden Streets, beginning in 1852, the Spring Garden Institute instructed Baldwin apprentices in mathematics and industrial crafts. Further to the east, the modest homes of the workers crowded onto the narrow blocks created by John Penn during his development of Northern Liberties in the 1790s.[5]

As noted earlier, the Philadelphia and Reading had leased access to the Delaware and Schuylkill Railroad west to Broad Street and had constructed a passenger station at Broad and Cherry Streets in 1839. In 1850, the P&R purchased the Delaware and Schuylkill line that it was using to access its Broad and Cherry Street station, and in 1857, the right-of-way east of Broad Street to the Delaware, where

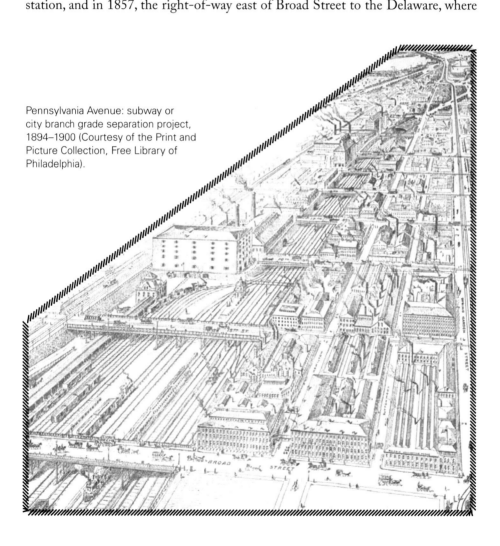

Pennsylvania Avenue: subway or city branch grade separation project, 1894–1900 (Courtesy of the Print and Picture Collection, Free Library of Philadelphia).

the track had been operated as the Northern Liberties and Penn Township Railroad. The P&R rebuilt its tracks and developed extensive wharf facilities on its Delaware River frontage, and a new passenger station at Broad and Callowhill Streets in 1861. The docks brought the P&R into contact with John Henry Towne's North Pennsylvania Railroad, extending from Bethlehem 57 miles to its tidewater station "Cohocksink" at the foot of Willow Street, and serving Josiah White's anthracite mines in the Lehigh Valley.[7] In 1878, the P&R leased the North Penn, but it remained in existence as a letterhead company and continued to own scraps of property throughout its former system, as the author discovered during real estate development projects.

With the Willow Street Line and the North Penn converging at the docks at the foot of Willow Street, the Philadelphia and Reading had assembled what by late-19th-century standards must have been considered a sophisticated, multimodal terminal that benefited the industries located at Bush Hill, providing them with ready access to domestic sources of raw materials and to foreign and domestic markets for their products. The North Penn's line in the bed of American Street was soon faced with factory rail sidings as Philadelphia, by then known as "Workshop of the World," attracted industrial development with its excellent rail and water logistics and its proximity to suppliers and customers, as well as the technological expertise concentrated in the American Philosophical Society and the Franklin Institute. The P&R boasted that it had more industrial sidings per mile of running track than any other American railroad, and this unmatched concentration of freight activity was on display every day on American, Noble and Willow Streets.

As ocean shipping technology progressed, and iron and steam replaced wood and sail, ships grew in size to a point where the Philadelphia port's narrow channel and short piers created a serious impediment to its international commerce. The city successfully lobbied the federal government to deepen and widen its river channel (see Chapter 7), removing two islands in the process. Philadelphia's Board of Port Wardens followed up with construction of large, modern piers, the first of which, the magnificent 570-foot-long Pier 19 North, was located adjacent to the P&R Willow Street piers and the Noble Street Freight Station, as the Cohocksink Station was then called. Pier 19 is now a restaurant and the original P&R piers 24, 25 and the double-decked Pier 27 North, with tracks on both its upper and lower floors, are now shorn of their superstructures, remaining as parking lots.

While the Delaware and Schuylkill Railroad had been constructed on an unbuilt canal right-of-way, its tracks met the existing surface grade of adjacent lands and streets, and the area that it occupied was designated by the city as Pennsylvania Avenue as far east as Broad Street, although the presence of numerous tracks and switches in its bed likely meant that its use as a city street for pedestrian and carriage traffic was precluded. However, its level grade with its surroundings required numerous railroad-street crossings, notably at Broad, Spring Garden and Green

Streets. The rapid industrial, rail-intensive development of Bush Hill, coupled with the fashionable residential development of the Spring Garden district and below Callowhill Street, generated public outcries to resolve the traffic congestion, especially at Spring Garden Street, the neighborhood's gateway to Fairmount Park and the scenic Water Works, a major tourist attraction. The issue came to a head in the late 1880s when the Baltimore and Ohio Railroad proposed to link the P&R's Pennsylvania Avenue Line with their Philadelphia-Washington Line then under construction (see Chapter 3), and they negotiated an agreement with the city to construct that connection in a tunnel, below the grade of the adjacent streets.

John Evans' Sons, Inc. (Author's photo). This building predates the lowering of 13th Street's grade, as can be seen by the second-floor doorway.

Beginning in 1888, the city and the P&R entered into negotiations, culminating in a March 17, 1894 ordinance providing for a sharing of costs to depress the tracks in an open cut below street grade from a point between 21st and 22nd Streets east to Broad Street. West of 22nd Street, the P&R placed its tracks in the tunnel constructed jointly with the Baltimore and Ohio Railroad, and known thereafter as the subway, to just northwest of Fairmount Avenue, topped with Pennsylvania Avenue. This combination of subway tunnel and open cut allowed the railroad to continue service to its Hamilton Street Freight Depot at the southwest corner of 20th and Hamilton Streets and the line's industries with its steam locomotives whose emissions precluded extending the subway further east. The city raised Broad Street above the grade of the track and depressed 13th Street below it.[7] Further east of 13th Street toward the Delaware River, the track in the beds of Noble Street and Willow Street remained at grade with the surrounding properties, and traces of it can still be found there. Around this time, the 1.4 miles of tracks east of Broad Street began to be called the Willow Street Line, or the Willow and Noble Street Line, and the 1.5 miles of track west of Broad became the City Branch or Subway Branch.

The remarkable story of Matthias Baldwin and his Bush Hill locomotive works follows the trajectory of the American railroad industry from its beginnings to its zenith in the first decade of the 20th century and to its steady decline thereafter. From its first seven orders received from the Philadelphia and Columbia Railroad, output rose to 37 units in 1850, to 259 in 1870, and to 2,648 in 1880, with a corresponding increase in Baldwin employment from 400 in 1850 to 18,500 by 1907, all accommodated on 17 acres of land on which were constructed 64 acres of floor space. Baldwin maintained and increased productivity by building and rebuilding its factories, often vertically by adding floors, while still maintaining production and constantly improving machinery and equipment. Drawings for new machinery such as overhead electric cranes would be drafted by Baldwin engineers, patents would be applied for, and the drawings would be shopped to Baldwin's neighbors Bement & Dougherty or William Sellers & Son for fabrication. Baldwin installed Edison incandescent electric lighting in 1881, doubling work shifts to 24 hours, and added electric motors in the 1890s.[8]

During the first decade of the 20th century, the American locomotive industry produced almost 43,000 engines, and Baldwin accounted for 39 percent of them. With 40 percent of its output destined for export, Baldwin truly was an international industrial giant. In 1906, the year of its greatest output ever, Baldwin made its first purchase of lands in Eddystone, Delaware County, anticipating that the boom in locomotive orders would go on indefinitely, but its timing could not have been worse as the railroad industry never fully recovered from the Panic of 1907 or from the 1906 Hepburn Act, which gave the Interstate Commerce Commission authority over railroad rate increase requests. Eddystone achieved full size in 1928, when Baldwin shuttered its Bush Hill shops, but with its 600 acres of land and 100 acres

Baldwin locomotive on Sellers turntable. Preston Retreat is in the background (Courtesy of The Library Company of Philadelphia).

of floor space, docks for ocean vessels on the Delaware River and access to the Pennsylvania and B&O Railroads, the site never operated at more than 30 percent capacity during peacetime. Five years later, it produced just 23 engines, the company's lowest output since 1848. Baldwin finally abandoned locomotive building in 1956, and three years later donated the 1876 Centennial Exhibition replica of its very first industrial engine, *Old Ironsides,* to the Newcomen Society, who gave it to the Shelburne Museum in Vermont.

As the 20th century dawned, the American economy began to shift away from what has been called the first Industrial Revolution—smokestack industries of coal, iron, steam and textiles—and toward a second one of oil, autos, steel and electricity. If Matthias Baldwin was the symbol of the first revolution, Edward G. Budd (see Chapter 7) would be Philadelphia's symbol of the second. The effect of this second revolution on the Willow Street Line and Bush Hill would be profound.

By 1942, the old Bush Hill industrial district could hardly be recognized. Baldwin had completed demolition of its properties there in 1937, and most of Bush Hill's other industries were gone, too. Their sites were either vacant or now occupied by warehouses of supermarkets and department stores, harbingers of the arriving distribution economy, or by firms such as I-T-E Imperial, a manufacturer of electrical

It was over, over there. Baldwin World War I victory parade float with *Old Ironsides* replica and Preston Retreat in the background. *Old Ironsides* was Baldwin's first commercially viable locomotive, sold to the Philadelphia, Germantown and Norristown Railroad. Baldwin attempted to acquire this locomotive for the 1876 Centennial Exposition, but was not able to locate it, and then built this replica. After leaving the locomotive business in the 1950s, Baldwin donated the replica to the Newcomen Society, which gave it to a museum in Shelburne, Vermont. Endowed in 1836, Preston Retreat (at the northeast corner of 21st and Hamilton Streets) was one of America's first maternity hospitals, and is now a division of Pennsylvania Hospital. This photo was taken from one of William Sellers' machine shops (Courtesy of The Library Company of Philadelphia).

transformers, and Smith, Kline & French and the nearby Sharp & Dohme, pharmaceutical companies that did not use rail service but required a better-educated workforce, portending a future knowledge-based economy. At least the warehouses generated some traffic for the Reading, as it was called by then, but not nearly as many jobs for neighboring residents as the manufacturers formerly on these sites. The site of Bement & Dougherty Machine Works was now a playground. Today, about the only vestige of that bygone locomotive era is to be seen at 506 North 13th Street, the John Evans' Sons machine shop, mostly unoccupied except for its ground floor, now used as a stable and barn for the horse-drawn carriages that transport tourists around Independence Mall and Society Hill.

Baldwin's move to Eddystone must have been a profound economic and professional loss for the Philadelphia and Reading Railroad. After all, every bill of lading for a delivered Baldwin locomotive identified the P&R as the originating carrier. The railroad set about trying to find new rail customers for the vacant sites along its Willow Street Line, and one of its first moves was to convey its freight yard at the northwest corner of Broad and Callowhill Streets, formerly used to service Baldwin, to the Elverson family, who owned *The Philadelphia Inquirer* and who could be counted upon to be a large and steady railroad customer. The Elverson Building, designed by Rankin, Kellogg & Crane and completed in 1924, is a memorable Italian Renaissance structure faced with white terra-cotta details and rising in a series of setbacks to a graceful central clock tower.[12] The Elversons conveyed their old headquarters, adjacent to Reading Terminal on Market Street, to the railroad, which constructed an annex to its headhouse offices there. *The Inquirer* expanded its operations in Bush Hill during the 1940s, occupying most of Baldwin's Broad Street frontage with its rotogravure plant and another press in what had been one of the buildings on the Hoopes & Townsend factory site. Other printing businesses gravitated to Bush Hill, taking advantage of its empty properties and rail access for their paper supplies. An example is the Lasher Printing Company, with a plant designed by Philip Tyre; in 1927, Lasher constructed its Art-Deco building at 1309 Noble Street, where a portion of Hoopes & Townsend had stood. Most recently, *The Inquirer*'s operations in the Elverson Building have moved back to Market Street and the building will be converted to a hotel.

Opposite the Elverson and Lasher buildings, the Reading Railroad constructed its massive, 13-story, multi-tenant Terminal Commerce Building, 401 North Broad Street, at its completion reputed to be the largest warehouse, office and showroom building of its kind in the eastern United States, and housing a railroad yard and freight station in its basement. This yellow brick and light-brown terra-cotta structure with Egyptian ornamentation was designed by William Steele & Sons and built in 1930.[12] Along the north elevation of this building can be seen the dining car that marks the location of the Willow Street Line. It has fed lunch to generations of workers from the adjacent Inquirer, Terminal Commerce and Lasher buildings.

Further east of 13th Street, where the line met the grade of the adjacent streets and properties, the neighborhood originally known as Northern Liberties and Penn Township still retained its Colonial era character of narrow streets and small building sites with mixed industrial, commercial and residential uses on practically every block. One might think that such a constrained location might not be conducive or economical for rail freight operations, but as recently as 1959, the intensity of rail activity there was remarkable.

In August 1959, the Philadelphia City Planning Commission completed a study of railroads in Philadelphia with respect to their facilities and operations and their impact on city planning. This report undertook a case study of economic linkages between freight transportation and other phases of economic activity. The railroad freight station that they chose for this close examination was Noble Street, at the foot of Willow Street opposite the Reading's Pier 27 North, at the location of the North Penn Railroad's 19th-century Cohocksink Station.[11]

The Planning Commission study found Noble Street Station to be one of the Reading's busiest, servicing six substations, four of which were located along Philadelphia's Delaware waterfront, and two elsewhere on the Willow Street Line, at 5th and Willow Streets and at 2nd and Master Streets. Noble Street Station was one of the Reading's chief centers of trucking activity as well. Altogether, this station served 529 freight customers within a three-and-a-half-mile radius, shipping 120 products ranging from peanuts to trucks.

In 1959, a typical urban railroad freight station such as Noble Street would have served three main functions: delivery of railcars over the street railroad tracks to customers' private sidings; delivery of railcars to public sidings, known as "team tracks," located at Noble and its six substations, where the customers would load and unload the railcars themselves; and loading and unloading of customers' merchandise within the station's building for pickup or delivery by the railroad's trucking company or by a private trucking company to the customers' location or for the customers' own pickup at the station. While the author never visited Noble Street Station in its heyday, he can recall riding in his uncle's truck to a Reading team track in Olney and watching workers using a manual pallet jack to unload building materials from a boxcar.

Of Noble Street Station's 529 customers in 1959, 108 were manufacturing firms employing over 13,000 workers, and 238 firms received delivery of railcars at their private sidings. About half the companies used the team tracks, primarily those at the Noble Street Station, although 60 used a substation. The Planning Commission study found that the customers were dispersed in a fan shape along Delaware Avenue, and the linkages between the freight station and other business activities were numerous, varied and active.

The Planning Commission study described the Willow and Noble Street Branch in 1959 as varying between two and four tracks to the Reading Company piers at the foot of Callowhill Street, on the Delaware River, and including a fairly extensive series of yards, freight stations and team tracks at 8th, 5th and Willow Streets. The line was connected with Reading Terminal at 11th and 12th Streets, and experienced occasional passenger rail service. It passed at street grade from 12th Street to the Delaware River, with all intersecting streets crossing at grade. The line was constructed of girder rail in the beds of streets, permitting truck and automobile use of the same areas as occupied by the tracks. It wound between the various industrial, warehouse and loft buildings that lined its route, sending off sidings to those buildings as well as to freight stations spaced approximately three blocks apart. The conflict between train movements and the street vehicular traffic was very great, and traffic on the north-south intersecting streets was frequently delayed. The numerous street crossings necessitated very slow operations of the trains and locomotives, and there were often serious difficulties involving trains, parked freight cars, parked trucks and vehicular traffic on Willow and Noble Streets. The narrowness of the right-of-way in places, the restricted clearances alongside tracks, the crowding of the sidings, and the sharp radii of some of the curves on the sidings seriously impaired the efficiency with which the line could be operated. Keeping grade crossings of intersecting streets clear of railroad rolling stock, in accordance with state laws, necessitated much additional switching and locomotive movement. It must have been a very chaotic scene.

The line served the principal warehouse, light manufacturing and wholesaling district of Philadelphia and was a very important facility in the 1950s as it was the closest freight-carrying railroad line to the commercial core of Philadelphia, passing through an intensely developed area. Within 15 years, however, all of this railroad activity east of Broad Street had disappeared, the Reading Railroad was in bankruptcy, and the Willow Street Line did not even merit discussion in the U.S. Railway Association's Preliminary System Plan of lines to be considered for retention or abandonment after the bankrupt railroads were reorganized. The primary cause of this disappearance was construction of Interstate 95 through Philadelphia's waterfront, destroying the center of what had been the Noble Street Station's customer base. Another cause was urban renewal, whose definition of slums and blight no one could argue failed to apply to Willow and Noble Streets in the early 1960s, but it must also be noted that those areas of Northern Liberties that escaped "urban renewal" are today's ground zero for Philadelphia's current gentrification revival.

The urban renewal answer, in the form of redevelopment plans for the Franklin Town and Callowhill Urban Renewal Areas west and east of Broad Street, had no provision for freight trains operating on city streets. Reading's successor Conrail continued to operate freight trains on the below-grade City and Subway Branch in Bush Hill to *The Inquirer,* the City Branch's sole remaining customer until that firm relocated its printing plant to the suburbs in 1992, after which Conrail ended service.

The Reading fell into bankruptcy in 1971, a victim of the dramatic decline in its primary traffic commodity, anthracite, after World War II, overregulation and increased truck competition resulting in part from construction of the interstate highway system. In 1942, German submarines had come close to choking off coastal petroleum shipments from the Texas Gulf to the refineries of the Northeast, many of which were along the Delaware River, home to the second largest concentration of petrochemical refining in the United States. This prompted the federal government to ration petroleum-based fuels and initiate construction of pipelines northward and out of the submarines' threat, with a major junction of these pipelines in Philadelphia near the refineries. After the war ended, residents quickly discovered that this now readily available and low-priced liquid hydrocarbon was far easier to transport and use than the anthracite that heated their homes. Anthracite carloadings plunged on the Reading as it raced to find alternative freight business, but the effort was too little and too late to save it.[7]

The problem of ICC overregulation of transportation was belatedly recognized and addressed in the decade after the Reading's bankruptcy, as one by one the trucking, air, rail and ocean transport industries were deregulated. Passage of the Railroad Revitalization and Regulatory Reform Act in 1976 and the companion deregulatory Staggers Act in 1980 are significant reasons for the rail industry's resurgence since then, with profitable carriers in 2010 moving double the volume of 1980s freight on schedule at rates just a fraction of what they were in the 1970s. The railroads also learned how to use the interstate highway system to their advantage for moving freight intermodally in containers carried by any imaginable combination of railroads, trucks and ships.

Mauch Chunk's fortunes also rose and fell with Josiah White's anthracite mines in the Lehigh Valley, and by the early 1950s, it was abundantly apparent that the mines were in trouble. As unemployment mounted, Mauch Chunk's residents decided to create a fund to lure industries that would create jobs for the "Chunkers." Alas, the fund failed to attract any takers, and so the town hit on another idea—tourism. Fate intervened with the coincidental death of Jim Thorpe, a Native American Olympic gold medal winner and outstanding football player from Oklahoma. Chunkers approached his widow with the proposition that if Thorpe were to be buried in their town, they would apply their industrial development fund toward creating a memorial suitable for him, as well as change the name of their town to Jim Thorpe.

Jim Thorpe, the town, has prospered with tourism, but the attraction is not Jim Thorpe, the monument. It is the mansions of coal barons, the jail that held the riotous anthracite miners known as the Molly Maguires, the pretty town that would look right in place in the Tyrolean Alps, the white water rafting on the Lehigh, the bike trails along remnants of Josiah White's canal, the majestic Pocono Mountain scenery and the Josiah White–inspired model gravity and scenic railroads that draw visitors to this seat of aptly named Carbon County. At this writing, the family of Jim Thorpe, the athlete, has filed a lawsuit demanding the return of his remains for reburial in his native Oklahoma, contending that his final repose on Bear Mountain has become unrestful. Perhaps the tourists disturb him. This lawsuit has plunged the Chunkers into an identity crisis. After all, what would Jim Thorpe be without Jim Thorpe? One Chunker, Mike Allen, owner of a psychedelic-themed coffee shop, has offered an original suggestion: rename the town Jim Morrison, an idea that no doubt would inspire the late rocker to give a hearty shout-out of his approval. But the town that now thrives on having discovered that its future lies in its past could do a lot worse than to rename itself Josiah White.[13]

References

1. George H. Burgess and Miles C. Kennedy, *Centennial History of the Pennsylvania Railroad* (Philadelphia: The Pennsylvania Railroad, 1949), provides an account of George Washington, Robert Morris, canal building in Pennsylvania and New York, the development and sale of the Main Line of Public Works and the creation of the PRR.
2. Jay V. Hare, *History of the Reading* (Philadelphia: John Henry Strock, 1966), is a collection of articles that first appeared as a serial in *The Pilot* and in *Philadelphia and Reading Railway Men,* beginning in May 1909 and ending in February 1914. The account includes stories of the construction and operation of the Schuylkill Canal and Philadelphia and Reading Railroad, and a biography of William Sellers.
3. Russell F. Weigley, ed., *Philadelphia: A 300-Year History* (Wayne, PA: The Barra Foundation, 1982), includes discussions of the yellow fever epidemic, Stephen Girard and the development of the Water Works.
4. Edward Arthur Mauger, *Philadelphia Then and Now* (San Diego: Thunder Bay Press, 2002), details the founding of the American Philosophical Society.
5. Agnes Repplier, *Philadelphia: The Place and the People* (New York: Macmillan, 1898), is an account of the founding of Philadelphia and of early life in the colony.
6. Rudolph J. Walther, *Happenings in Ye Olde Philadelphia, 1680–1900* (Philadelphia: Walther Printing House, 1925), is the story of Josiah White's discovery of anthracite ignition, mining development in Mauch Chunk, and the source of statements that "The Delaware and Schuylkill Railroad was practically the first passenger railroad within the City of Philadelphia" and that "The Northern Liberties was the sixth largest American town in 1800." This book is a treasure of information on early life in Philadelphia.
7. James L. Horton, *The Reading Railroad: History of a Coal Age Empire, Vol. 1: The Nineteenth Century* (Laury's Station, PA: Garrigues House, Publishers, 1989), is an account of the early development of the P&R along the "Little Schuylkill"; biographical information on Hiester, List, Girard and Robinson; a survey of the route to Philadelphia; acquisition of the Northern Liberties and Penn Township Railroad and the North Penn Railroad; passenger station development in Philadelphia; and the life of P&T employee and artist David J. Kennedy.
8. John K. Brown, *The Baldwin Locomotive Works: A Study in American Industrial Practice* (Baltimore: The Johns Hopkins University Press, 1995), contains a history of Baldwin's rise and fall in Bush Hill and Eddystone; Baldwin's role in the economy, production and employment levels, and railroad industry conditions; an account of the Hepburn Act and the ICC; a comparison of the first and second Industrial Revolutions, epitomized by the locomotive and automobile industries; and descriptions of other manufacturers located in Bush Hill.
9. *The Encyclopedia Americana,* 1955 edition, contains inventor biographies and the history of the steam engine.
10. Francis Burke Brandt and Henry Volkmar Gummere, *Byways and Boulevards In and About Historic Philadelphia,* Sesqui-Centennial Souvenir Edition (Philadelphia: Corn Exchange National Bank, 1925), recounts travelers' experiences on the Belmont inclined plane and a description of John Fitch's steamboat experiment; it also provides a period map of central Philadelphia.
11. Philadelphia City Planning Commission, *Philadelphia Railroads* (Philadelphia: PCPC, Comprehensive Planning Division, 1959), includes a case study of Noble Street Freight Station.

12. Federal Writers' Project, Works Progress Administration, *WPA Guide to Philadelphia* (Philadelphia: University of Pennsylvania Press, 1937; reprinted 1988), provides descriptions of the Elverson and Terminal Commerce buildings, Spring Garden Institute and Samuel Vauclain's purchase and relocation of the Japanese Pagoda to Fairmount Park.

13. "Is There Life After Jim Thorpe for Jim Thorpe, Pa.?" (*The Wall Street Journal,* July 21, 2010) reports on the Thorpe family lawsuit to return Jim Thorpe's remains to Oklahoma.

14. *The Independence Square Neighborhood* (Philadelphia: The Penn Mutual Life Insurance Company, 1926), includes an account of the design and construction of Independence Hall.

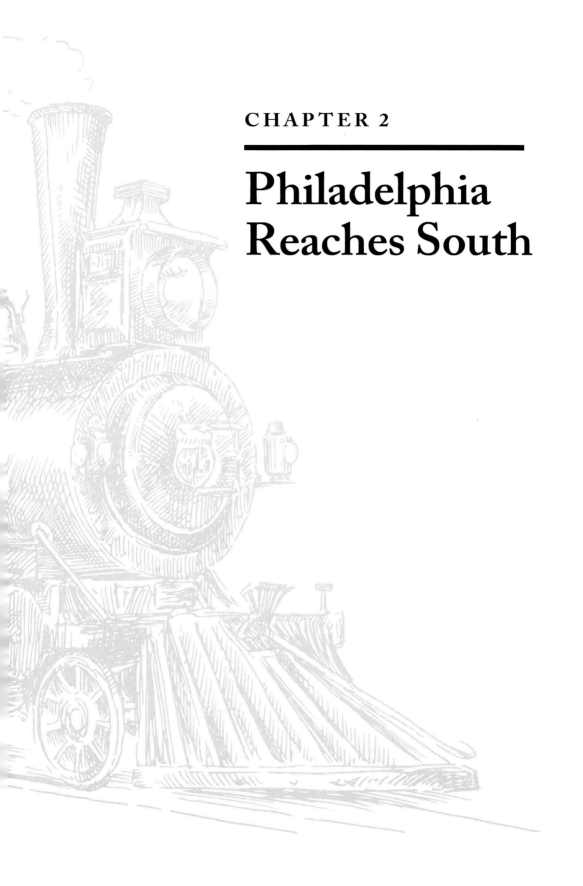

CHAPTER 2

Philadelphia Reaches South

n Amtrak's Acela, the trip from Philadelphia to Washington takes an hour and 39 minutes, including stops in Wilmington and Baltimore, and the Acela attains speeds of up to 150 miles per hour. In Colonial times, the trip only as far south as Baltimore could take three days, and travelers were few. Sailing along the Atlantic coast was the preferred route, as the Colonies' population centers were concentrated there. Since they were dependent on commerce with Britain and other overseas markets, the need for north-south transportation was minimal, and bodies of water on or near the coast, such as the Long Island Sound, the Hudson and Santee Rivers, Delaware River and Bay, and the Chesapeake Bay were much preferred for travel among the Colonies.[1]

Colonial annals record citizens' petitions to legislatures, pleading for road construction, but they also contain their complaints of the approved roads' surveyors having chosen routes that favored their friends, family and business partners at the petitioners' expense, and outrage over the lack of maintenance on what roads already had been constructed. Bridges were almost nonexistent, requiring fords, which gave these early routes a zig-zag pattern from one shallow stream crossing to the next. Notable roads of that era included the 1748 King's Road from Philadelphia to New Castle, Delaware, where it veered inland to an eastern tributary of Chesapeake Bay, for a boat trip the final 45 miles to Baltimore. The King's Road was the established north-south route until well after the Revolutionary War, when it became known as the Southern Post Road or the Philadelphia Plank Road, later the Darby Road, with the portion within Philadelphia coming to be named Woodland Avenue. George Washington made this three-day trip many times.

The first extensive improvement of an American highway occurred in Pennsylvania, when the 62-mile Philadelphia-Lancaster Turnpike was paved with crushed stone in 1795. The period when Philadelphia was the national capital saw numerous turnpike and canal projects proposed and shortly thereafter under way, but by the 1830s, changing technology clearly favored railroads, and turnpike companies began converting their rights-of-way to this new alternative.

One of these first conversions happened in 1829, when the New Castle and French-town Turnpike Company added "and Rail Road" to its name. Construction of the 16-mile-long railroad was opened with steam locomotive power in October 1832. In April 1831, the Pennsylvania legislature authorized creation of a railroad from Grays Ferry, on the west bank of the Schuylkill River in Philadelphia County, southward to the Pennsylvania-Delaware state line. In January 1832, the Delaware Assembly authorized incorporation of the Wilmington and Susquehanna Rail Road Company, followed by Maryland's approval of the Delaware and Maryland Rail Road Company in March. These three end-to-end railroads consolidated, in February 1838, to form the Philadelphia, Wilmington and Baltimore Railroad, which began construction on July 4, 1835, and inaugurated service on Christmas Day, 1838.

While this railroad spanned three states, it was very much a Philadelphia creation. A preliminary survey and cost estimate for its construction was undertaken by a young civil engineer, J. Edgar Thomson (1808–1874), future president of the Pennsylvania Railroad during the height of its expansion period (1852–74). Benjamin Latrobe, Jr. (1806–1878), son of the designer of Philadelphia's original Centre Square Water Works, was in charge of the Baltimore-Havre de Grace section. His father's former student, William Strickland (1787–1854), managed the Wilmington to Susquehanna River segment, and Samuel Kneass (1802–1858), Strickland's former student, engineered the Philadelphia to Wilmington segment, including reconstruction of the Grays Ferry Bridge, renamed the Newkirk Viaduct to honor Matthew Newkirk (1794–1868), the first president of the consolidated railroad. The Newkirk Viaduct Monument was erected to celebrate the railroad's completion, and the names of Philadelphians Newkirk, Strickland, Latrobe and Kneass can be found on the work. This neglected, graffiti-stained, 30-foot obelisk can be found along the Amtrak Northeast Corridor and seen from the Grays Avenue overpass at 49th Street.[1][11]

The PW&B's Newkirk Viaduct, a combined rail and highway bridge, gave it access to Moyamensing Township (or District) on the east bank of the Schuylkill,

The Philadelphia, Wilmington and Baltimore Railroad's Newkirk Viaduct, spanning the Schuylkill River at Grays Ferry, opened for service on Christmas Day, 1938. This combined railroad and highway bridge remained in service until 1902, when the PRR's subsidiary, the Philadelphia, Baltimore and Washington Railroad, constructed the present bridge. It was left abandoned in the position open to river traffic, and can be seen below the current Grays Ferry Avenue Bridge (Courtesy of PhillyHistory.org, a project of the Philadelphia Department of Records).

and it extended its track along what was then Prime Street, now Washington Avenue, as far east as Broad Street. There it connected with and soon purchased a short railroad, the Southwark, allowing it to continue eastward to the docks on the Delaware River and Philadelphia Naval Shipyard, and northward on Broad Street to South Street, then the southern boundary of the city, giving the PW&B access to the commercial district that Philadelphians call Center City. From South Street, its cars switched onto the horse-drawn municipal railroad for the final travel to the PRR passenger station at 11th and Market Streets or the P&R station at Broad and Callowhill Streets.[1] [2]

Philadelphia and other large cities proscribed steam engine operation, ostensibly out of fear of fires being started by flying sparks, but a more mundane reason may have been that the delayed traveler might just prefer to stay in town for the night and spend his money on local room and board. The PW&B had to have its trains hauled by horsepower through Wilmington, and this practice continued in Baltimore until well after the Civil War. Today railroads operate through cities, but a remnant of this old practice can still be seen in Chicago, where most freight railroads terminate on the outskirts of the city and their trains must be switched to continue their journey—a major headache for the operators. The Chicago Area Transportation Study has kept planners employed for decades.

The PW&B had figured out a solution to crossing the Schuylkill, but crossing the much broader Susquehanna was a different matter altogether. For many years, it relied on steamships for the crossing, first its *Susquehanna* and later its *Maryland*. Passengers were required to walk from the track terminus to the dock, board the steamer, and then depart on foot on the other side to reach the waiting train. The steamer had rails on its second deck to accommodate the baggage cars, thus arguably creating the first car ferry, but the preference the railroad gave to its freight was not lost on its passengers.

The PW&B, like Pennsylvania's Main Line of Public Works, was exposed to the vagaries of weather because of this Susquehanna crossing, which could become impossible because of ice or storms. In the winter of 1851–52, it even built an "ice bridge" of track laid on the surface for passage of its trains from January 15th to February 24th, when the spring thaw commenced. An actual bridge over the Susquehanna was not completed until after the Civil War.

The PW&B solved its horse-drawn railroad problem in Philadelphia with construction of a new passenger station at Broad and Prime Streets, where Moyamensing Township allowed steam engines, in 1852. The passenger station, resembling Milan's La Scala opera house, was used until 1881, when Broad Street Station began operations, and survived until the early 1960s, when it was demolished by the federal government to create a metal shed. The PW&B's adjacent freight station continues in use today as a warehouse, whose owner is proud of the history of his building, listed in the National Register.

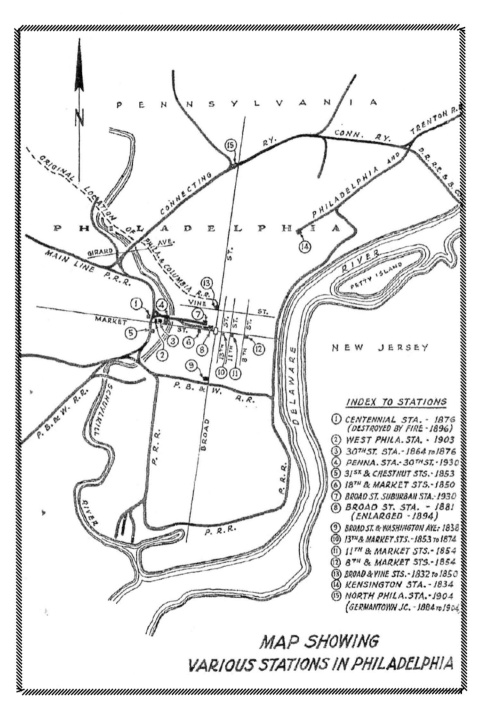

INDEX TO STATIONS

1. CENTENNIAL STA. - 1876 (DESTROYED BY FIRE - 1896)
2. WEST PHILA. STA. - 1903
3. 30TH ST. STA. - 1864 to 1876
4. PENNA. STA. - 30TH ST. - 1930
5. 31ST & CHESTNUT STS. - 1853
6. 18TH & MARKET STS. - 1850
7. BROAD ST. SUBURBAN STA. - 1930
8. BROAD ST. STA. - 1881 (ENLARGED - 1894)
9. BROAD ST. & WASHINGTON AVE. - 1838
10. 13TH & MARKET STS. - 1853 to 1874
11. 11TH & MARKET STS. - 1854
12. 8TH & MARKET STS. - 1854
13. BROAD & VINE STS. - 1832 to 1850
14. KENSINGTON STA. - 1834
15. NORTH PHILA. STA. - 1904 (GERMANTOWN JC. - 1884 to 1904)

MAP SHOWING
VARIOUS STATIONS IN PHILADELPHIA

The Pennsylvania Railroad in Philadelphia. The terminal farthest south, on the east bank of the Schuylkill River, is Girard Point. The line extending eastward from it, known as the Delaware Extension, leads to the Delaware River at Greenwich Point (Courtesy of the Pennsylvania Historical and Museum Commission and the Railroad Museum of Pennsylvania).

The tracks along Washington Avenue were the subject of major reconstruction and realignment in the 1950s, and remained in active rail operation until the early 1970s, finally being paved over in the 1980s. The Philadelphia City Planning Commission's 1959 study, *Philadelphia Railroads,* identified 185,340 carloads handled in 1956 on the Pennsylvania Railroad's southern section, which encompassed their Broad and Washington, Grays Ferry and Paschall Stations. This amounted to 28 percent of all PRR traffic in Philadelphia that year. All this activity is gone, memorialized today only by the odd angle of a wall here or there in what is now a loft condominium complex, reflecting where a rail siding once led to a factory or military depot.[10]

It is not difficult to imagine the strategic value that the Philadelphia, Wilmington and Baltimore Railroad must have had in the Civil War, how much the federal government depended on it as the middle link between New York and Washington to ferry troops and supplies to the Virginia battlefields. It was one of the North's four north-south railroad lines, and the only one connecting Philadelphia and the northeastern states with the South. In 1861, railroads were still a patchwork arrangement, with gaps between them. There was no railroad connecting Philadelphia directly with cities farther north; instead the "United Railroads of New Jersey" linked Newark and New York Harbor with Trenton, from which one line extended south to Kensington in Philadelphia County. Another of the United Railroads, the Camden and Amboy, terminated across the Delaware River. Passengers arriving by ferry from Camden usually made the walk from there to the PW&B station at Broad and Prime Streets, although carriages were available, but the trip from Kensington Depot took much longer, as it was across the city from the PW&B station. The passengers' ride ended at the PW&B's President Street Station in Baltimore; they then continued on foot or in horse-drawn carriages along Pratt Street for over a mile through the city to the Camden Street Station of the Baltimore and Ohio Railroad for the final leg of their journey to Washington.[1 2]

While Philadelphia Quakers and Mennonites had protested the institution of slavery vigorously in the years leading up to the outbreak of the Civil War, many Philadelphians, like other Americans, were gripped with ambivalence about South Carolina's stated intent to withdraw from the Union. Philadelphians had strong ties to the South. Southern buyers purchased a large share of Philadelphia's manufactured goods, and Baldwin and Norris locomotives were on every Southern rail line. Many planters maintained homes in the city—22 on one block of Walnut Street alone[3]— and Pierce Butler, one of South Carolina's largest slaveholders, maintained an estate, "Butler Place,"[4] in Olney. His grandson, Pierce Butler, Jr., was said to be Margaret Mitchell's model for the character Rhett Butler in *Gone with the Wind.* The anthracite tonnage moving over the Philadelphia and Reading Railroad's Port Richmond wharves exceeded the foreign tonnage of the Port of New York, and much of that anthracite was southbound. In 1838, rioters torched the just-completed Pennsylvania

Newkirk Viaduct Monument at 49th and Grays Avenue (Author's photo).

Hall and sent its anti-slavery supporters fleeing to the Quaker village of Plymouth Meeting. In 1855, the American or "Know Nothing" Party, holding its national convention in Philadelphia, adopted a pro-slavery platform for the 1856 election. Its local candidate, Robert Conrad, was elected Mayor of Philadelphia. When John Brown's body arrived on the PW&B in 1859, accompanied by an honor guard of abolitionist leaders including Philadelphia's James Miller McKim, it was met by pro-slavery protesters at the Prime Street Station. In early 1861, many Philadelphians were under the impression that the breakup of the Union could never happen, that no majority in any state could be that foolhardy, but they misjudged the anger that many Southerners felt toward the rest of the nation, in part for thwarting their attempts to extend slavery into the new territories won in the Mexican War, and the extent to which that anger was now singularly focused on the newly elected President. Abraham Lincoln had earned the largest number of votes in a four-way race, but his victory was along geographic fault lines. In Baltimore, he won just four percent of the popular vote, and Baltimore was 500 miles north of Charleston.[37]

On December 16, 1860, a massive rally of Philadelphia's pro-Southern conciliationists, calling themselves the Silver Grays, convened at Independence Square to extend an olive branch of concessions to the South. The event's speakers assured the attendees that the majority of Southerners were not inclined to secede, but four days later South Carolina voted to take itself out of the Union. On January 9th, artillery batteries in Charlestown Harbor opened fire on the *Star of the West,* a merchant ship bringing supplies and reinforcements to the federal garrison at Fort Sumter, forcing the ship to withdraw. Six other states followed South Carolina in secession, forming the Confederate States of America in Montgomery, Alabama, and electing Jefferson Davis president on February 18th, two weeks before Abraham Lincoln's inauguration.

Having already received threats, on January 30th, PW&B president Samuel Morse Felton, Sr. summoned Chicago detective Allan Pinkerton to Philadelphia and hired him to safeguard the railroad. One of Pinkerton's agents, Timothy Webster, fell in with a gang of highwaymen at Perryman, Maryland, and overheard them discussing a plot to attack President Lincoln, wreck his train and murder him on his way from Harrisburg to Baltimore. They knew his itinerary and planned to ambush him when he traveled from Harrisburg on the Northern Central Railroad. Lincoln arrived in Philadelphia on the evening of February 21st to attend a flag-raising event at Independence Hall the following morning on Washington's birthday, celebrating the January 29th admission of the free state of Kansas into the Union. On the evening of his arrival, the President was met by Pinkerton and railroad executives who warned him and his entourage about the plot. Lincoln insisted on traveling to his appointment in Harrisburg later on the 22nd, but reluctantly agreed to return to Washington via Philadelphia and the PW&B line. Just before the Northern Central train on which Mr. Lincoln would have been traveling left the Harrisburg depot, employees of the American Telegraph Company there shorted the signal wire. No dispatches would go out of Harrisburg that night. Lincoln's closed carriage traveled from Harrisburg to Philadelphia on the Pennsylvania Railroad, proceeded over the horse-drawn municipal railroad to the PW&B's Prime Street Station, and was connected to an awaiting train. It was stated that the special car was for an "invalid gentleman." So carefully was this arranged that none of the railroads' employees knew that Mr. Lincoln was aboard. At six a.m. on February 23rd, Felton received a telegram from Washington, informing him that the President had arrived safely. Lincoln's February 22nd speech at Independence Hall, his raising the Stars and Stripes, and the pomp and circumstance surrounding the event earned him his first real popularity in Philadelphia; until that event, he had generally been regarded as an uncouth frontiersman. The good will and admiration that the President earned on February 22nd would be sorely needed in the trying days ahead.[3][6]

On April 9th, South Carolina militia artillery lieutenant William Stuart Simkins ordered his Charleston battery to open fire on Fort Sumter, thus beginning

Pennsylvania Railroad Station at 11th and Market Streets (Courtesy of the Germantown Historical Society, Philadelphia, PA).

the Civil War. On the 15th, President Lincoln called on Pennsylvania for 16 regiments of volunteers, and Philadelphians responded with enthusiasm. On the 19th, a unit of Philadelphia recruits, the "Washington Brigade," without either weapons or uniforms, boarded the PW&B for Baltimore and Washington. The train was preceded by an armed and uniformed Massachusetts regiment, which was attacked by a mob in Baltimore and suffered three fatalities and 17 injuries as it marched through the streets to the B&O station. The Philadelphians behind them were then set upon by the mob, which had been persuaded by local newspapers that Maryland was being invaded. On April 22nd, Private George Leisenring, a native of Germany who lived in Fishtown, died at Pennsylvania Hospital in Philadelphia, succumbing to a stab wound to the thorax inflicted on him in Baltimore, and becoming the first Philadelphian to die in the Civil War.[3]

The situation in Baltimore now approached chaos. More than any other city, Baltimore had embraced the "Know Nothing" Party, which had plied its brand of mob rule, pressure politics and anti-immigrant, anti-Catholic rhetoric before the war. The rise and fall of the "Know Nothings" were both ephemeral. Horace Greeley of the *New York Tribune* noted that the party "contained about as much of the elements of permanence as an anti-cholera or anti-potato-rot society."[8] But after it had faded elsewhere, the Know Nothings managed to hold onto power in Baltimore by dividing the spoils of government among the gangs who supported them. Clearheaded, rational statesmen they were not. After the attack on the Philadelphia recruits, Maryland's Know Nothing governor, Thomas H. Hicks, proclaimed, "I love my state and I love the Union, but I will suffer my right arm to be torn from my body before I will raise it to strike a sister state." He and the Mayor of Baltimore,

Passenger station of the Philadelphia, Wilmington and Baltimore Railroad. Located at the northwest corner of Broad and Prime (Washington Avenue) Streets, and known as the Southern and Western Station, it was in use until 1881, when the PRR's Broad Street Station opened. After that time, the station was used as a freight terminal, and was finally demolished by the federal government in 1964. The original PW&B freight house, seen to the right of the passenger station, survives and is used as a food distribution warehouse. The funeral cortege train returning to Springfield, Illinois, stopped at Broad and Prime Streets, and Abraham Lincoln's body lay in state at Independence Hall after his April 1865 assassination (Courtesy of PhillyHistory.org, a project of the Philadelphia Department of Records).

George W. Brown, jointly sent a telegram to President Lincoln, asking that no Federal troops be sent through the city. When Lincoln delayed in replying, the governor, mayor and police chief met and arrived at a remarkable way to solve the troubles pressing in on them. They would prevent Federal soldiers from entering Baltimore by destroying all the railroad bridges to the north and east. The reader's imagination can only conjure what must have been taking place in the final moments of this meeting.[7]

This destruction was placed in the hands of a former superintendent of the PW&B, Isaac Trimble. On April 20th, he burned the PW&B bridges over the Harris Creek in Baltimore and the Bush River Bridge. On the 26th, he sent the long Gunpowder River Bridge up in flames. All telegraph wires leading from Baltimore were cut. It required 24 days of hard work to repair the damage. After April 1861, the only further damage to the PW&B occurred on the morning of July 14, 1864, during a raid conducted by Lieutenant Colonel Harry Gilmor's 2d Maryland Cavalry, part of General Jubal Early's Shenandoah Valley force, which had broken through the Federal army's blockade of the valley after the Confederate victories at New Market and Monocacy, and was on its way to menace Washington, D.C.

Gilmor positioned two captured trains on the Gunpowder River Bridge and then burned the lot. The otherwise relative lack of damage to this important route during the war can be attributed to the Federal declaration of martial law in Maryland, but also to the PW&B's own 200-man force of bridge guards. A train was kept in readiness to concentrate them at any time, and in order to allay any suspicion, they were kept at work whitewashing the bridges, some of which were given six or seven coats, a good protection against fire.[1 9]

The Baltimore and Ohio Railroad, the southernmost of the rail links between New York Harbor and Washington, took the full brunt of wartime disruption. Its route to the Ohio River and the West took it through the Potomac River Valley, one of the prizes sought by the Confederates; its bridge at Harper's Ferry burned five times, and often whole sections of the railroad would be out of the management's control for weeks and even months as the tide of battle ebbed and flowed across the Potomac. Just one month into the war there occurred the "Great Train Raid" led by Confederate General Thomas Jackson of future "Stonewall" fame. With the South having little capacity to manufacture locomotives, rails or rolling stock, Jackson was ordered to seize as much of this material as possible, and he devised a plan to capture

Abraham Lincoln in Philadelphia. On February 22, 1861, President-elect Lincoln attended a flag-raising event at Independence Hall's State House, celebrating the admission of free-state Kansas into the Union. He stopped in Philadelphia on his way to Harrisburg (Courtesy of The Library Company of Philadelphia).

rolling stock by tearing up B&O tracks between Point of Rocks, Maryland and Cherry Run, in what is now West Virginia. Jackson made off with nine miles of rails, tools and a complete turntable, but a subordinate's mistake in prematurely burning a bridge put their haul of locomotives, materials and rolling stock in jeopardy. Jackson then organized a convoy of horses, mules and oxen to pull the railroad equipment on specially made "trucks" along the Shenandoah Valley Turnpike to Staunton, where they were reassembled and put on tracks to Richmond. Tactically, this remarkable Confederate feat electrified the residents of the Shenandoah Valley and brought many recruits to the rebel cause, but strategically, it was a blunder as Jackson now had antagonized a powerful and heretofore uncommitted observer of this growing conflict—the president of the B&O Railroad, a man who was rare to show anger, but one who would eventually and always get even.

The B&O was fortunate to have as its chief executive officer John W. Garrett (1820–1884), who had the knowledge, patience and political skills to keep the railroad from totally disintegrating under the pressure of war. Garrett shared the instincts of Governor Hicks and many other Marylanders to avoid this war by any means possible, and the tact to keep his enemies at either a distance or a minimum. But now that Jackson had drawn the B&O into the fray, Garrett's honor required

John W. Garrett (From the author's collection).

that there be no turning back. Garrett had known Edwin McM. Stanton, Esq., from earlier times when Stanton was a rising young attorney in Pittsburgh before being appointed to President Buchanan's cabinet in December 1860. As Buchanan's Attorney General, he had been the most committed unionist in the cabinet, and had frustrated efforts by the Secretary of War and his Southern colleagues to recall the *Star of the West* from its voyage to Fort Sumter, thus redeeming the closing days of Buchanan's otherwise passive, lackluster presidency. President Lincoln recognized Stanton's talents and instincts, and appointed him Secretary of War. Garrett now cultivated his acquaintance with Stanton until it grew into a friendship that expanded until it included Abraham Lincoln as well. Garrett pledged Lincoln his full cooperation, and Lincoln gave him his trust. Unlike other railroads that were seized by the military, the B&O remained under its own management throughout the war. Instead of being told what to do, Garrett was asked. Had he remained neutral, the B&O would have been commandeered and Garrett himself fired, if not arrested. After President Lincoln's assassination, it was John W. Garrett who organized his friend's funeral train home to Springfield, Illinois, with stops in major Northern cities, including Philadelphia at the PW&B's Broad and Prime Street Station.[7]

Of Garrett's many wartime problems, the greatest was that his railroad ran along the border of North and South. For a few miles, people living along the line might be totally pro-Union, but a few miles beyond it, entirely for the rebels. Confederate commanders took advantage of this, raiding and cutting the lines not once but hundreds of times. Garrett understood that the B&O response had to be organizational, not political. His solution was to create a workforce whose loyalty was not to South or North, but to the B&O. His employees treated the burning of bridges, the destruction of track, the theft of locomotives and rolling stock, and the deliberate derailing of trains as a normal day at work, something to be dealt with, just as they would a flood or an accident or lost baggage.

During the April-May 1861 temporary loss of the burned bridges, the Federal army adopted the alternative of using the PW&B ferry *Maryland* as a troop ship to sail down the Susquehanna and occupy Annapolis, the capital, ostensibly as a rail depot to get troops through to Washington after the bridges were destroyed. The Maryland House of Delegates, fleeing to Frederick, denied that it had no right to pass an ordinance of secession, and began debating whether to leave the Union. If Maryland withdrew, Washington, D.C., surrounded by the Confederacy, would be an untenable place for the Federal government, and it would have to withdraw, perhaps back to Philadelphia. On the night of May 13th, a Federal force commanded by General Benjamin Butler arrived in Baltimore from Annapolis, took over Federal Hill, trained its artillery across the basin at the heart of the city, and proclaimed martial law. General Butler arrested the mayor, the chief of police and Baltimore's delegates to the state legislature, locking them up in Fort McHenry, which locals were now calling the American Bastille.

Baltimoreans were picked up and interrogated selectively and randomly, then confined in the fort. Among the many caught up in the Federal dragnet were Francis Key Howard, grandson of the author of "The Star-Spangled Banner," and Severn Teackle Wallis, a member of Maryland's House of Delegates and future chancellor of the Maryland Bar Association, on neither of whom the irony of their confinement would have been lost. U.S. Supreme Court Chief Justice Roger Brooke Taney, himself a Marylander, traveled to Baltimore to issue a writ of habeas corpus for one of the prisoners, only to have it ignored by the commanding officer of Fort McHenry. Governor Hicks was promoted out of mischief's way, the reincarnated Republican appointed to the United States Senate, where the Lincoln Administration could keep a closer eye on him in Washington. Desperate times called for desperate measures.[7]

During the course of the war, the Philadelphia, Wilmington and Baltimore transported hundreds of thousands of troops, returning casualties, thousands of freight carloads of materiel, and not a few Confederate prisoners—a strategic asset in the Federal government's long-term ability to sustain the fighting. The war also generated significant retained earnings for the PW&B, and with the arrival of peace, it sought to fund improvements to its lines. In its southern territory, the railroad finally built a bridge over the Susquehanna. On its northern end, the PW&B's original right-of-way had bordered the Delaware River rather too closely from Grays Ferry in Philadelphia to Chester, with the result that track flooding became an ongoing problem. After the war, the PB&W shifted its right-of-way further west and north, out of the floodplain and onto what is now the alignment of Amtrak's Northeast Corridor. Later, a swing bridge crossing the Schuylkill was constructed, replacing the Newkirk Viaduct. This newer swing bridge can still be seen in Grays Ferry, south of the Grays Ferry Avenue Bridge, permanently left in the position open to river traffic, as its use for Conrail freight was terminated in the 1970s. The PW&B then sold its flood-prone former line to Chester to the Philadelphia and Reading Railroad in 1871, after which it was renamed the Chester Branch. This branch has been shifted several times since then as Philadelphia International Airport has developed. A middle portion of it is used as the Philadelphia International Airport High Speed Line, with the Conrail Shared Assets Organization continuing freight service on either end for CSX and Norfolk Southern, its owners. The author participated in a track relocation project there in 1986, preparing a site for development of the United Parcel Services air terminal along the Delaware River and Hog Island Road. During this project, he discovered a half-mile segment of what may have been the original PW&B inside the airport fence along Tinicum Island Road, near the intersection of 2nd Street and 4th Avenue in the town of Lester. Unlike the modern ribbons of continuous welded rail that railroads now install, this overgrown track was composed of 39-foot lengths of steel rail attached end to end with bolted joint bars, with each rail stamped with the year of its manufacture. What little remained of the wooden ties underneath them crumbled to the touch. An inspection of a sample of those rails indicated that they were manufactured in the 1870s.[2]

For the most recent development on the old PW&B segment in Philadelphia, CSX has improved and created double-stack container height clearance on a small section of its Grays Ferry end, between 49th Street and Eastwick Junction, below 51st Street in the vicinity of the Newkirk Viaduct Monument, as a link in its Jacksonville-to-Montreal route. CSX picked up this track segment during its acquisition of Conrail jointly with Norfolk Southern.

Before the Civil War, Philadelphia could be described as a railroad hub with poorly connected spokes. The Philadelphia, Wilmington and Baltimore ended at Broad Street and Washington Avenue, the Philadelphia and Reading at Broad and Callowhill Streets, the Philadelphia and Trenton in Kensington (at Front and Berks Streets) and the Pennsylvania Railroad at 11th and Market Streets. What tied them together was the city's horse- and mule-drawn railroad system of "string teams" towing freight and passenger cars in the beds of Broad and Market Streets. The vast increase in freight traffic in the 1850s made this system intolerable even when it ran 24 hours a day.[1][2]

Strangely, Philadelphia's own anti-immigrant and anti-Catholic riots of May and July 1844 were to have a far-reaching impact on the city's rail network, and ultimately on the future development of all railroads serving the city and region. These riots occurred in the outlying Philadelphia County districts of Kensington and Southwark, not directly within the city limits as those boundaries existed at that time. The extent of the resulting deaths and destruction—with the burning of Catholic churches, convents and libraries and the use of militia weapons seized from arsenals during the carnage—convinced civic leaders that the township governments were unequal to the task of providing security and that governance within Philadelphia County had to be restructured. In the May riot in the county's Kensington district, the only police officer available had been the sheriff, and in July, 5,000 militiamen were needed to put down the outbreak in Southwark.[5] Thus was born the popular agitation that resulted in the 1854 consolidation of the city and county governments, with the original city government taking responsibility for the policing and public administration of the various former townships.

It soon became apparent that the existing City Hall building adjacent to Independence Hall was far too small to manage its greatly increased responsibilities, and the city's leadership determined to erect a much larger headquarters. Alternatives included building a structure at each of the city's five squares or a single structure at either Centre or Washington Square.[12] A site alternatives committee recommended and voters approved that it be located on Centre (or Penn) Square, at Broad and Market Streets, but this was also the location of the interchange yard for the municipal mule-drawn railroad system. Considering that Washington Square was the burial site of many Revolutionary War soldiers, the voters' choice of Centre Square was predictable. Another alternative would need to be found for the railroad junction, as construction of City Hall was approved by City Council on April 17, 1872. The first stone of the new structure was laid on August 9th, and its cornerstone was dedicated on July 4, 1874. The Connecting Railroad and the Junction Railroad were the Pennsylvania Railroad's alternatives to Centre Square junction, proposed by that Machiavellian genius, J. Edgar Thomson (1808–1874), president of the PRR from 1852 to 1874.[1]

The Connecting Railroad's premise was to avoid the inefficiency and delay of the Centre Square rail junction and link the PRR's 30th Street (West Philadelphia) yards directly with the United Railroads of New Jersey's Philadelphia and Trenton terminus at Kensington Avenue and Berks Street by constructing a new bridge across the Schuylkill near the Philadelphia Zoo (Zoo Junction), and then a 6.4-mile-long track arching across North Philadelphia to a connection with the Philadelphia and Trenton in Frankford (the PRR's Frankford Junction). The connecting route would skirt

J. Edgar Thomson (1808–1874), surveyor of the Philadelphia, Wilmington and Baltimore Railroad (1835) and president (1852–1874) of the Pennsylvania Railroad during its period of greatest expansion (Photo from the *Centennial History of the Pennsylvania Railroad*, reprinted with permission from the Pennsylvania Historical and Museum Commission and the Railroad Museum of Pennsylvania).

around to the north of the most heavily developed former townships. The agreement to build this route, signed in February 1863, gave the PRR a through route from anywhere on its east-west system to Jersey City and the New York Harbor. It also permitted the Philadelphia and Trenton Railroad access to a new PRR passenger station in West Philadelphia, to be built in 1864 on the approximate location of today's 30th Street Station, and to another proposed connection called the Junction Railroad that was at the same time being negotiated with the PW&B and the P&R on the west bank of the Schuylkill. Completed in 1867, the Connecting Railroad created a completely locomotive-powered route linking New York, Philadelphia and Pittsburgh, and not a moment too soon. In 1869, the Pennsylvania Railroad leased the 468-mile-long Pittsburgh, Fort Wayne and Chicago Railway, which became the PRR's gateway to the West and established it as America's premier long-distance railroad. In 1872, construction of Philadelphia's City Hall began.

Also avoiding Centre Square, the Junction Railroad proposed by President Thompson for the west bank of the Schuylkill River would greatly increase the strategic economic value of the PW&B. If it could be linked directly to the Connecting Railroad, it would provide a route joining New York, Philadelphia, Wilmington and Baltimore, and no longer would have to interchange traffic on the city's municipal railroad. Planning for the Junction Railroad began in 1860, involving a 1.3-mile-long link northward from 30th Street, completed in 1863, to a junction with the Philadelphia and Reading at their Columbia rail bridge at the foot of the old Belmont Plane, and a 1.66-mile connection southward, finished in 1866, from 30th Street southward to a junction with the PW&B near the Newkirk Viaduct. The three-party agreement (PRR, P&R and PW&B) was interpreted by the Pennsylvania Railroad to mean that the Junction Railroad would pass over the PRR's 30th Street tracks rather than own them, but its partners contested this, wanting a completely independent and neutral route through the PRR yards. The

The Pennsylvania Railroad's 31st Street Station (1864), terminus of the main line and midpoint of the three-mile Junction Railroad (Courtesy of the Germantown Historical Society, Philadelphia, PA).

dispute went into the courts and was finally settled in the PRR's favor. On the Junction Railroad, the fox was now minding the chickens.

In 1871, the PRR leased the United Railroads of New Jersey, giving it not only control of its rail lines over that state, but also of its Trenton Delaware River rail bridge and the Philadelphia and Trenton Railroad with its rights under the Connecting Railroad agreement. But the fox was still hungry.

The Pennsylvania Railroad's acquisition of the New Jersey lines was undoubtedly regarded unfavorably by the Baltimore and Ohio Railroad, one of the PRR's chief competitors for east-west freight since that fateful vote in the Pennsylvania legislature in April 1846. The B&O, via the PW&B, had indirectly benefited from the completions of the Junction (1866) and Connecting (1867) Railroads, but with its rival now controlling the New Jersey railroads, the B&O was in a vulnerable spot. Its president, John W. Garrett, decided to take the war to the enemy's turf, especially after the PRR created delays and obstacles to its trains on the 30th Street section of the Junction Railroad. Garrett's plan was to gain control of the Philadelphia, Wilmington and Baltimore, but first he had to apply some muscle. He arranged for his friends in the Delaware legislature to approve a charter for a new railroad, the Delaware and Western, which would essentially parallel and compete with the PW&B. Believing discretion to be the better part of valor, PW&B's management approached John Garrett with a counterproposal for him to acquire a controlling interest in their stock, represented at this meeting by their largest shareholder, Nathaniel Thayer of Boston. The negotiated price was $70 per share. In a rare lapse of discretion, President Garrett, the guest of honor at a large Boston dinner party, boasted that he had arranged the purchase of a majority of the PW&B stock and that in a few days it would pass into his possession. This news was immediately communicated by one of the diners to George B. Roberts (1833–1897), president of the PRR from 1880 to 1897. Within a few days, Roberts let it be known to the shareholders that his offer was $78. The majority of them accepted that offer on March 7, 1881.[1] [2]

This was dire news for John Garrett, because the Pennsylvania Railroad now also owned the PW&B's share of the Junction Railroad; sure enough, he notified the Baltimore and Ohio that they would refuse to transport any B&O trains on either of them. Although a court battle ensued, the PW&B's (or one should now say, the PRR's) position was sustained. The B&O had to build its own line to Philadelphia. The fox feasted.

The story of the Philadelphia, Wilmington and Baltimore Railroad ends with its purchase by the PRR. All that remains of it in Philadelphia are its historically certified freight shed on the northwest corner of Broad Street and Washington Avenue, now used for the distribution of Asian foods, and the graffiti-covered Newkirk Viaduct Monument along the Amtrak tracks near 49th Street and Grays Ferry Avenue. It does not reflect well on the railroads serving Philadelphia to have that memorial to the city's railroad history left in such a deplorable state. It is not as though the railroads are ignorant of it. After all, Amtrak and SEPTA trains pass it every day, and the monument's location and significance are specifically noted in Joseph F. Folk's landmark study of the Philadelphia Terminal, so there is no excuse for Conrail, CSX and Norfolk Southern to be unaware of it. One hopes that the Newkirk Viaduct Monument will not only be restored and protected, but better yet relocated to a site where people can actually see and appreciate it, and read its inscriptions. This author believes that Amtrak's 30th Street Station would be an ideal location at which to display the monument, as both it and the elegant station celebrate Philadelphia's remarkable role in American transportation history.

References

1. George H. Burgess and Miles C. Kennedy, *Centennial History of the Pennsylvania Railroad* (Philadelphia: The Pennsylvania Railroad, 1949), discusses colonial transportation; the construction and operation of the Philadelphia, Wilmington and Baltimore Railroad; the Junction and Connecting Railroads; the purchase of the United Railroads of New Jersey and the Philadelphia, Wilmington and Baltimore; the lease of the Pittsburgh, Fort Wayne and Chicago Railroad; and the Pennsylvania Railroad in the Civil War.

2. J.V. Hare, *History of the Reading* (Philadelphia: John Henry Strock, 1966), originally appeared as serialized articles in *The Pilot* and *Philadelphia and Reading Railway Men*, beginning in May 1909 and ending in February 1914. It covers Philadelphia's municipal horse-drawn railroad, Reading's perspective on the dispute with Pennsylvania Railroad regarding the Junction and Connecting Railroads, and the B&O's attempted purchase of the PW&B and its eventual purchase by the PRR.

3. Frank H. Taylor, *Philadelphia in the Civil War* (City of Philadelphia, 1913), discusses Philadelphians' prewar attitudes toward slavery, abolition and secession; the Baltimore riot and the death of Private Leisenring; the attempted assassination of President Lincoln in early 1861; and the PRR in the Civil War.

4. Marita Krivda Poxon, Rachel Hildebrandt and the Old York Road Historical Society, *Images of America: Oak Lane, Olney and Logan* (Charleston, SC: Arcadia Publishing, 2011), includes a discussion of Butler Place.

5. Dennis Clark, *The Irish in Philadelphia: Ten Generations of Urban Experience* (Philadelphia: Temple University Press, 1973), includes a description of the Philadelphia "Know Nothing" riots.

6. Federal Writers' Project, Works Progress Administration, *WPA Guide to Philadelphia* (Philadelphia: University of Pennsylvania Press, 1937), discusses Philadelphians' reaction to President-elect Lincoln's speech at Independence Hall on February 22, 1861.

7. Hamilton Owens, *Baltimore on the Chesapeake* (New York: Doubleday, Doran and Company, 1941), covers prewar Baltimore politics; the decision to set fire to rail bridges; the arrests of the mayor, the police chief, and Maryland delegates and other citizens; an account of the B&O during the Civil War; and John W. Garrett's friendship with President Lincoln.

8. *The Encyclopedia Americana*, 1955 edition, includes a discussion of the American ("Know Nothing") Party; Philadelphia city-county consolidation; the Know Nothing riots in Philadelphia; President Buchanan and War Secretary Stanton; the secession of the Confederate states; and the attack on Fort Sumter.

9. Virgil Carrington Jones, *Gray Ghosts and Rebel Raiders* (McLean, VA: EPM Publications, 1984), includes an account of Lt. Col. Gilmor's burning of Gunpowder River Bridge in July 1864.

10. Philadelphia City Planning Commission, *Philadelphia Railroads* (Philadelphia: PCPC Comprehensive Planning Division, 1959), discusses rail traffic volumes and patterns in 1956.

11. Joseph F. Folk, *The Philadelphia Terminal: A Description of Penn Central's Freight Operations in a Major Urban Terminal* (Philadelphia: Penn Central Transportation Company, 1973), discusses the location and significance of the Newkirk Viaduct Monument.

12. Rudolph J. Walther, *Happenings in Ye Olde Philadelphia, 1680–1900* (Philadelphia: Walther Printing House, 1925), gives an account of the site determination of City Hall.

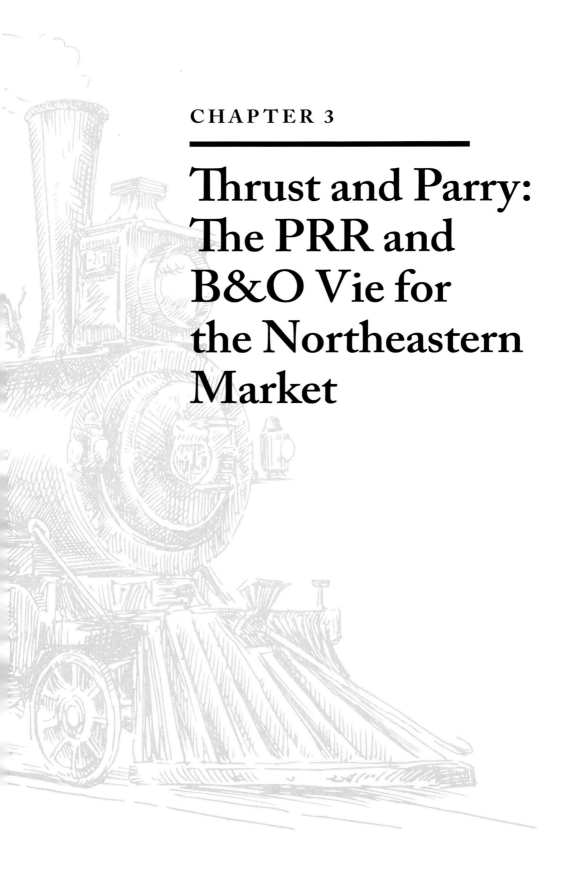

CHAPTER 3

Thrust and Parry: The PRR and B&O Vie for the Northeastern Market

he north-south railroad transportation network serving the Mid-Atlantic states in 1861 was a vast improvement over the Post Road of 30 years before, but there were significant gaps within cities, with the railroad stations often being on the outskirts of town where the rail lines terminated. These gaps were caused by opposition to their extension into built-up areas, or to the expense of constructing these extensions, or by cities preferring that the railroad lines not connect, so that the passengers might spend some time and money in town before traveling on. The gaps within cities left opportunities for improvement that were easy for railroad engineers and entrepreneurs to imagine.

In 1861, the Pennsylvania Railroad, then primarily an east-west carrier, did not own one foot of rail in the corridor between the New York Harbor and Washington, D.C., and the Baltimore and Ohio Railroad owned only the one segment known as its Washington Branch Rail Road from Baltimore's Camden Street Station into Washington. The remainder of this corridor was owned by the Philadelphia, Wilmington and Baltimore Railroad, the United Railroads of New Jersey, and the various municipal street railroads in Philadelphia, Wilmington and Baltimore, who treated through or "overhead" traffic of the other railroads with impartiality—or, as some passengers and shippers might complain, indifference. From its rail yards on the west bank of the Schuylkill River near Market Street, the PRR accessed the PW&B to its south, and to its north the Philadelphia and Reading Railroad and the branch of the United Railroads reaching Philadelphia, known as the Philadelphia and Trenton Railroad, by way of the city's mule-powered street railroad system running down the centers of Broad and Market Streets. These connections were extremely inefficient. The B&O, another east-west carrier, likewise used the PW&B and the Philadelphia municipal railroad to pass its overhead traffic on to the United Railroads' Philadelphia and Trenton Railroad, inaugurating its B&O Jersey City-to-Washington passenger service in December 1863, the trip taking 10 hours. The B&O also used Philadelphia's horse-powered municipal railroad for traffic interchange with the P&R at their terminal at Broad and Vine Streets.

If the PW&B and the United Railroads were impartial regarding other railroads' traffic, the B&O certainly was not, as it denied the PRR through ticketing and baggage checking arrangements at Baltimore for travel south on its Washington Branch subsidiary. This was B&O spite, pure and simple, arising from the intense competition that the railroads engaged in and the residue of that fateful April 1846 vote in the Pennsylvania legislature, denying the B&O access to Pittsburgh.

Perhaps because the Baltimore and Ohio's attentions were focused more on the Civil War's exigencies than the Pennsylvania Railroad's, when the PRR began its maneuvers to enter the north-south business in a more controlling way, the responses of the B&O were the proverbial "day late and dollar short." The B&O may have felt annoyance with the PRR's Junction (1866) and Connecting (1867) Railroad projects in Philadelphia, and concern with its 1869 lease of the 468-mile-long Pittsburgh,

Fort Wayne and Chicago Railway. But annoyance and concern turned to shock and horror when in June 1871, the PRR leased control of the United Railroads and announced, in those pre-regulatory days, that henceforth it would refuse to carry over this line any B&O traffic having its origins at points in the west in common with the PRR. Accordingly, all such B&O western traffic would have to be turned over to the PRR in Pittsburgh. The effect of this turn of events would be to end the B&O's drive into western markets and relegate it to a role of a local trunk railroad operating between Baltimore and Wheeling. This was an unbearable outcome, an unimaginable setback, a totally unacceptable situation to befall the B&O.

The PRR, however, was not yet finished with humiliating the B&O, for it had even more serious trouble planned for its archrival. The B&O enjoyed a Washington, D.C. traffic monopoly on its Washington Branch Rail Road, which had been granted it by the Maryland legislature in return for a 20 percent tax on the branch's passenger revenues. Perhaps it was complacency with this apparent monopoly that tempted the B&O to treat its PRR business with such prejudice. The PRR now employed astute Maryland counsel to research possible legal alternatives to the Washington Branch, and they found one in a long-dormant charter giving the Baltimore and Potomac Rail Road Company rights to build a line from Baltimore to Pope's Creek in the general vicinity of Bowie, but with the stipulation that none of its branches could exceed 20 miles in length. This provision was thought to protect the B&O monopoly, in the belief that no branch from Pope's Creek could ever reach Washington within 20 miles, but its author had not reckoned on the capabilities of the PRR survey corps. The Pennsylvania Railroad engineered a branch that took it into Washington within 16 miles of the Baltimore and Potomac Rail Road, whose charter the PRR had artfully purchased. This branch was now the center of attention, more valuable than its trunk line.

The Pennsylvania Railroad's Washington-Baltimore service began on this line in July 1872, breaking the B&O monopoly. Over the next year, the PRR plowed money into improving its new route, which cut through a densely developed area of Baltimore, and built its Baltimore station. In January 1874, following its lease of the United Railroads, the PRR announced that the same limitations that the B&O imposed on the PRR's Washington traffic would now apply to B&O traffic between Philadelphia and New York Harbor (Jersey City). Travelers between Jersey City and Washington would need only to ride on the PRR the entire way to avoid the B&O's inconveniences. On November 12, 1874, it was recorded that the ride on the PRR from its West Philadelphia station to Jersey City took one hour and 47 minutes, and the ride from that station southward to Baltimore took two hours and 15 minutes. At six hours and 40 minutes, the PRR's entire ride from Jersey City to Washington was not something that the B&O could match.[1]

This injury compounded with insult was more than B&O president John Garrett could stand. Garrett's first impulse was to bring legal action against the PRR for blocking his trains from using the Junction Railroad to move onto the

Philadelphia and Reading Railroad. The P&R had only recently come into possession of the North Penn Railroad, and so the B&O imagined creating a route alternative to the PRR by coming north on the PW&B, moving over the Junction Railroad at Grays Ferry to the P&R at Belmont Junction, then up the North Penn's Bound Brook route to northern New Jersey. The court, however, found in favor of the Pennsylvania Railroad, concluding for a second time that the PRR did in fact own the middle one mile of the three-mile Junction Railroad and could operate that as it pleased. When the B&O's train on the PW&B crossed onto the Junction Railroad, it was stopped so that the PRR could attach its locomotive to haul it the three miles to the P&R at Belmont Junction. While it was stopped, PRR conductors boarded and collected a 15-cent charge from each passenger for this junction service. None of this PRR activity was undertaken with any particular alacrity. In December 1880, the P&R brought suit against this unreasonable delay, but the issue became moot in March 1881, when the Pennsylvania Railroad purchased the Philadelphia, Wilmington and Baltimore.

Now entirely shut out of the New York Harbor–Washington corridor, the B&O scrambled to create an alternative connection to the P&R, as both the PW&B and the Junction Railroad were controlled by the Pennsylvania Railroad. First, the B&O used a small railroad, the Delaware and Western, which it had created in order to bully the PW&B, to form the nucleus of a competing route. Intermediate towns along this line were enthusiastic at the prospect of competition for their freight, and Wilmington passed the necessary ordinances in November 1882, providing the B&O with the needed right-of-way through the city. The B&O's construction schedule was set at half a mile per day with completion expected by July 1885, including bridges over the Susquehanna and Schuylkill.

As the new line approached Philadelphia, the B&O considered using the P&R's 11-mile-long Chester Branch, the PW&B's main line until sold to the Reading in 1871, but rejected this idea because of the line's history of flooding. Instead, in Pennsylvania, the B&O created a new subsidiary, the Schuylkill River East Side Railroad Company. The name emphasized its right-of-way on the east side of the Schuylkill, as the B&O knew that it would have no further hope of accessing the Junction Railroad on the west bank. The East Side Railroad would cross the Schuylkill on a drawbridge 2,000 feet south of what had become the PRR's Newkirk Viaduct. It proposed to undercut all streets in the central business district until it joined the P&R at 21st Street and Fairmount Avenue, a location to be called Park Junction, and to extend an at-grade line eastward in South Philadelphia to the Delaware River to access port traffic.

The B&O now faced the daunting task of securing the necessary right-of-way street crossing or street occupation ordinances from the PRR's hometown legislature. Their feeling must have been similar to Jonah's in the whale's belly, knowing that only faith and hope would see them through what was certain to be a long, dark, dank and thoroughly miserable experience. The role of Jonah would be played by the B&O's chief counsel, John K. Cowen (1844–1904), later president of the railroad (1896–1901) and a U.S. Congressman. In those days, Philadelphia City Council was a bicameral body, its parliamentarians divided into Select and Common Councils, and "observers" from the Pennsylvania Railroad could be found prowling the visitors' galleries, keeping a watchful eye on the proceedings. At that time, every one of the city's 50 wards elected its own councilman, and the opportunities for mischief in such a large legislative body were boundless. Even today, in a slimmed-down council of 17 members in a city of 66 wards, the federal correctional "country club" at Allenwood, to which all convicted Philadelphia politicians aspire to be sentenced, is sometimes called the "67th Ward" in homage to the city councilmen who have been confined there.

In the 1880s, councilmen had learned to recite from memory the list of grievances that the PRR had suffered in the hands of the B&O, and they loved to show off their knowledge before the gallery at every opportunity. The PRR wasted no time in pouncing. City Councils not only denied passage of the needed ordinances allowing the B&O to occupy or cross city streets, but they debated an ordinance instructing the City Solicitor to take appropriate action, by injunction or otherwise, to protect the city and adjacent private property owners being jeopardized by the B&O construction activity, and to prevent the B&O from building the railroad before City Council review and approval of their plans was obtained. Cowen protested that they had not begun building the railroad, but were only "filling in some swamps."

Railroad grade crossings were then, and still are, a major issue of contention. As initially proposed, the East Side Railroad was largely at grade except in Philadelphia's central business district, and thus generated particularly strong opposition from those residing in the Fairmount and Spring Garden neighborhoods north of it. They already were incensed by the P&R's activities on its freight line in the bed of Pennsylvania Avenue (discussed in Chapter 1), which physically obstructed the neighbors' access to Fairmount Park, Philadelphia's most pleasant recreation area, and to the beautiful Fairmount Water Works, 19th-century America's most-visited tourist attraction after Niagara Falls.[10] The B&O offered a compromise. If the city would elevate the grades of Green Street and Fairmount Avenue, the B&O would construct the city's street bridges and lower their own track, rendering access to Fairmount Park free of train obstructions at grade crossings.

The B&O was not without its Philadelphia supporters, who welcomed the prospect of another railroad competing for their freight business on the basis of better service and lower rates, in addition to buying supplies and providing more jobs. The Grocers and Importers Exchange, the Philadelphia Drug Exchange, the Philadelphia Produce Exchange, the Knights of Labor and the Carpenters' Assembly all testified in favor of the B&O. Eventually, special conditions were negotiated into an ordinance that City Council could accept, and the B&O was allowed to press forward, if only to be met with the anticipated blizzard of lawsuits. Delays and changes in plans caused B&O's actual costs to exceed original estimates by $4.5 million, a considerable sum at that time.

A major element of the project was the blasting of a tunnel through the rock formation beneath what was then the reservoir of the Philadelphia Water Department's Fairmount Water Works—now the site of the Philadelphia Art Museum. The tunnel extends from Filbert Street north to Fairmount Avenue, in what was then an already heavily built-up area of the city. Heated opposition to this blasting was further fueled by a contractor's misfire, which rained stones down on the neighborhood, injuring two women and penetrating roofs. This tunnel, the last work completed, provided space for an adjacent below-graded Philadelphia and Reading Railroad lead track to their Pennsylvania Avenue line, known henceforth as their "Subway" Branch, and allowed for the depression of this line below grades of crossing streets all the way east to Broad Street in the 1890s.[2][3]

The timing of the B&O–City of Philadelphia negotiations regarding this tunnel happens to coincide with the earliest references to planning a grand axial boulevard cutting across the city's gridiron street pattern from the formal entrance to Fairmount Park at Spring Garden Street southeastward toward City Hall. In 1884, Charles K. Landis, developer of Vineland, New Jersey, proposed this diagonal right-of-way, and in 1891, the city's director of Public Works, James H. Windrim, designed a plan for a boulevard 160 feet wide. This highway, today's Benjamin Franklin Parkway, first appearing on the city's plan in 1903, could not have been conceived with the P&R's tracks occupying Pennsylvania Avenue at street grade. Perhaps it is possible that the genesis of Philadelphia's own Champs Élysées may have occurred in the minds of the city's negotiators during their meetings with the B&O. Perhaps not.

The final span of the Baltimore and Ohio's Susquehanna Bridge was finished in May 1886, and the first train, carrying the president and other officers of the B&O, passed over the railroad from Baltimore to the western abutment of the new Grays Ferry rail bridge on May 11th. The completed Philadelphia-Baltimore route segment was put into operation for freight two months later. Passenger service from its new Philadelphia station at 24th and Chestnut Streets, designed in the Flemish Revival style by Frank Furness, was inaugurated on September 19th with three daily express trains in either direction. The patronage was quite gratifying, and almost immediately it was necessary to add three daily Philadelphia-to-Wilmington locals to accommodate riders who showed enthusiasm for the service. The connection with the P&R at Park Junction, in the vicinity of Pennsylvania and Fairmount Avenues, was finally completed, and the first New York passenger train went into service on December 15th. On March 10, 1890, it was recorded that the ride on the P&R from Philadelphia to Jersey City via Bound Brook took one hour and 25 minutes—that is, 22 fewer minutes than the November 1874 ride on the PRR between these two terminals.

The Baltimore and Ohio Railroad's Philadelphia Station. Designed in the Flemish Revival style by Frank Furness, it served the B&O's Philadelphia passengers from 1886 until 1963. The last scheduled passenger train departed on April 27, 1958 (Courtesy of the Print and Picture Collection, Free Library of Philadelphia).

The B&O provided passenger service between Washington and New York for 72 years, its final train departing its Philadelphia station on April 27, 1958. The station was demolished in 1963. It remained an active freight line, allowing the B&O and the Reading (and to their north, the New York Central) to compete with the PRR for cargo in the Mid-Atlantic states. Its supporters before City Councils were rewarded for their loyalty with competitive rail service in South Philadelphia and B&O investment over the years in local rail infrastructure. Examples include its extensive produce sheds, auction rooms and refrigerated warehouse, which it built in 1929 jointly with the Reading at the foot of Jackson Street, and its car floats at Piers

12 and 40 North to transport food products north to the Reading along the Delaware Riverfront. By then, the B&O had purchased a controlling interest in the Reading, and the operations of the two railroads were closely coordinated. In 1954, the B&O began converting some of its Jackson Street produce sheds and their adjacent tracks to handle Trailer-on-Flat-Car (TOFC) intermodal service, in competition with similar facilities developed around the same time by the Reading (initially at Wayne Junction and later at the Erie Avenue Yard) and the PRR (at the site of the original Philadelphia and Trenton Railroad station, and later at Meadows Yard, near Frankford Junction, and its mail van operation at the 52nd Street Yard). The Philadelphia City Planning Commission's 1959 study found that in 1956, the B&O accounted for 20 percent of all railroad carloadings in South Philadelphia.[7]

Ownership of both the Reading and the Penn Central passed to Conrail in 1976, during the regional rail reorganization, and it was not in Conrail's interest to encourage traffic with its east-west rival, then known as the Chessie System after a merger of the B&O, the Chesapeake and Ohio, and the Western Maryland Railroads. The former Reading line along the Schuylkill languished until Conrail's purchase in 1999 by CSX, successor to the Chessie System, and the Norfolk Southern, the latter once a subsidiary of the PRR. One of Conrail's early actions was to close the Reading and Penn Central TOFC and mail van terminals that it had inherited in Philadelphia and create a new facility in Morrisville, Bucks County. This was a considerable trucking distance from the port and the city's Food Distribution Center, although the Philadelphia Commerce Department and Planning Commission had urged Conrail to develop it at Greenwich Yard instead. Thus the city and port were dependent on the CSX TOFC terminal alone for convenient, lower-priced intermodal service for more than 20 years. When CSX took possession of the combined B&O-Reading line along the Schuylkill through Center City in 1999, CSX made it their principal route between Jacksonville and Montreal, and CSX has invested heavily in creating its Greenwich intermodal terminal as the city had originally recommended. After completing its Greenwich improvements, CSX sold its produce and refrigerated cargo terminal for shopping center redevelopment, and its last tenant, Delaware Avenue Distribution Company, relocated to Philadelphia's Food Distribution Center in 2003. With help from the Commonwealth of Pennsylvania, CSX has funded the considerable expense of improving its clearances to accommodate double-stacked containers on flatcars, coincidentally bringing double-stack and enclosed tri-level auto carrier capability on its line to the Port of Philadelphia, and traffic levels have increased considerably. Thus the logic of the B&O-P&R Schuylkill River Park Junction connection lives into another century.

The Pennsylvania Railroad formally consolidated the Philadelphia, Wilmington and Baltimore Railroad with the Baltimore and Potomac into a new company, triumphantly named the Philadelphia, Baltimore and Washington Railroad. This was in November 1902, at the time that the PRR built its new bridge over the Schuylkill, replacing the Newkirk Viaduct, and initiated extensive improvements to its terminal in Washington. It built a new "union" station in Baltimore in 1911, served by three PRR subsidiaries and the Western Maryland Railroad. Today this station is operated by Amtrak.

Prior to 1902, the Baltimore and Potomac had entered Washington, D.C. from the northeast, proceeding to a station opened by the PRR in 1873 at Sixth and "B" Streets, Northwest, and then on to cross the Potomac River on its "Long Bridge," used jointly with other railroads approaching from the south. The waiting room of this Washington station became infamous as the location where President James A. Garfield was mortally wounded on July 2, 1881 by Charles Guiteau, a disappointed office-seeker. Parts of this line were in the beds of city streets, so there were numerous at-grade street crossings, resulting in much public agitation to address the problem of Washington's traffic congestion.

In February 1901, Congress approved two acts directing the B&P and the B&O to eliminate all grade crossings and build new Washington stations. Both railroads were aware of the waste of duplicative facilities that would be built under these acts, which implicitly required separate passenger terminals. As a result, a third act, approved in February 1903, provided each company with a payment toward grade-crossing elimination and creation of a shared or "union" terminal. The station, completed in 1908, is a monumental granite structure in the style of nearby federal buildings. It was built and operated by the railroads' jointly owned Washington Terminal Company.[1]

In any story of the Philadelphia, Baltimore and Washington, mention should be made of the period during and immediately after World War I when the federal government nationalized the country's railroads under the auspices of an agency known as the United States Railroad Administration. In a massive undertaking, this agency commissioned surveys of every railroad property in the U.S. for the purpose of establishing the monetary value of the seized assets. These surveys, known as "Val Maps," today are used by surveyors, title companies and realtors alike. The Val Maps identify many properties in the Northeast Corridor as either owned by the PB&W, or more likely, with the PB&W in the chain of title.

The PRR's grand entrance onto Manhattan Island was celebrated with the opening of the magnificent Pennsylvania Station in 1910, but it was a long time coming. In 1899, the New York Central was the only east-west railroad to reach Manhattan without needing a water transfer across the Hudson River, as it crossed the Hudson on a bridge at Albany and came south on the river's east bank to its Grand Central Station at 42nd Street and Lexington Avenue. The PRR had extensive freight handling facilities on the West Side—piers and freight stations served by car floats from Jersey City—but its passenger service was at a distinct disadvantage, as travelers on the PRR to Manhattan could only go as far as Newark, and then had to board a ferry boat to the Manhattan station.

The concept of tunneling under the Hudson River, first proposed to the PRR in the early 1870s, had to await the development of a technological solution to the air pollution of the steam locomotive, and electricity was the answer. In 1884, Philadelphia's Franklin Institute hosted the brilliantly illuminated International Electrical Exhibition, containing 1,500 exhibits. It featured the application of electricity to printing presses, sewing machines, pipe organs—and the running of railroad trains.   Between September 2nd and its closing on October 11th, the Exhibition buildings, one of which was the Centennial Station recently vacated by the PRR upon its move to Broad Street Station, drew 285,000 visitors, and it is quite probable that among that number were PRR senior managers. By 1890, electric trolleys were operating on Philadelphia's Lehigh Avenue.[6] In 1904, Baldwin Locomotive Company and Westinghouse Electric Manufacturing Company jointly built their first electric locomotive, and on August 5, 1905, they announced that they had entered into a partnership to construct electric locomotives and develop a new electric railway system.[5] The PRR experimented with electric traction on the seven-mile-long Burlington and Mt. Holly Line in 1895, but abandoned it for commercial reasons in 1901. The first permanent railroad electrification project in the United States was undertaken by the B&O on their Belt Line in Baltimore in 1895. Its 3.63-mile route included a 7,300-foot-long tunnel. This was followed 10 years later by the Long Island Rail Road Company changing to electric operation.[4]

In 1901, Alexander J. Cassatt (1839–1906), director of the PRR from 1874 to 1882 and president from 1899 to 1906, attended the opening of the electrified extension of the Orléans Railway in Paris. He returned to Philadelphia convinced that this technology was the way to haul trains between Jersey City, Manhattan and Long Island. Perhaps he had also taken a ride on the Lehigh Avenue trolley. The project proposed by PRR's engineering department consisted of a double-track railroad starting from the main line east of Newark, crossing the Hackensack Meadows on a high fill, passing through Bergen Hill by separate single-track tunnels and under the Hudson River to 9th Avenue in Manhattan on two two-track tubes to Pennsylvania Station. East of the station, four single-track tubes extended east across Manhattan, with four tubes under the East River to a connection with the Long Island Rail Road at Long Island City. The station itself was designed for President Cassatt, brother of noted American impressionist artist Mary Cassatt, by the architectural firm of McKim, Mead and White. In pink granite marked by an imposing colonnade of Doric columns, its street frontage resembled Berlin's Brandenburg Gate.

If the B&O had been made to feel like Jonah in the belly of Philadelphia City Councils, the PRR's experience was akin to Daniel's in the lion's den of the New York Central's hometown and home state. The required street-closing or street-occupying ordinances and bi-state New Jersey-New York legislation needed to be secured, even though the project was underground at a grade of 93 feet below high water on the Hudson. The PRR persevered, and its imposing Pennsylvania Station stood as testimony to its grandeur and power until 1963 when it was demolished "in a monumental act of vandalism," according to *The New York Times,* and its debris dumped into the Meadows. This sacrilege gave impetus to the historic preservation movement in the United States. Among the few salvaged reminders of this beautiful structure are four of its granite eagles at each corner of Philadelphia's Market Street Bridge over the Schuylkill River at the former PRR, now Amtrak, 30th Street Station.

Passing on the opposite bank of the Schuylkill and under the eastern pair of these eagles, the B&O's East Side Railroad skirted industrial districts and operated through tunnels past residential and parkland areas of Central Philadelphia for its first 100 years. But beginning in the mid-1990s, interest began to grow in extending Fairmount Park southward as "Schuylkill River Park" along the ribbon of land below Filbert Street, between the East Side Railroad and the river's bank, as industry gave way to loft condominiums and planned unit developments brought in new residents. Once having lobbied for an extension of the park along the CSX right-of-way, the residents of the adjacent neighborhoods then wanted to improve their recreational access to it, just as the residents of Fairmount and Spring Garden had a century earlier. At this writing, it appears that a compromise has been reached regarding rail-crossing access points, which are for pedestrians and cyclists and at the grade of the active railroad tracks. Other cities and railroads have arrived at similar accommodations, and it is hoped that the compromise CSX and its neighbors have made holds as well as similar agreements elsewhere.

The American railroad industry peaked in the 10-year period beginning in the mid-1890s, after which it was hit with a series of vicissitudes from which it never recovered: nationalization during World War I, an Interstate Commerce Commission regulatory stranglehold on ratemaking and innovation, the Great Depression, the emerging efficiency of trucks, affordable air passenger transportation starting in the 1950s, and the loss of the U.S. Postal Contract in 1966, a particularly severe blow to railroad passenger service, on whose trains the postal cars were usually coupled. The PRR may have thought that, as the "Standard Railroad of the World," it could remain immune from these problems, but by the early 1960s, many problems were apparent. Its business base in the densely populated northeastern United States consisted of money-losing commuter and intercity passenger rail operations and labor-intensive short hauls of boxcar traffic that were particularly susceptible to competition from trucking. It was becoming less and less a railroad that originated freight, where the bulk of a railroad's revenue was earned, and more and more a terminating railroad, delivering traffic for the profitable long-haul lines such as the Burlington Northern and the Union Pacific for a share of revenue that might or might not fully compensate its costs. Its intercity passenger operations also were money losers, despite the PRR's investment in its high-speed Metroliner service along the Northeast Corridor. It continued to be profitable only because of its coal-hauling subsidiary, the Norfolk and Western, and paid dividends that it could not

The Eagle has landed. One of the eagles salvaged from Pennsylvania Station that grace the four corners of Philadelphia's Market Street Bridge over the Schuylkill River and the CSX tracks (Author's photo).

afford. A wave of mergers occurred in the industry in the early 1960s, and the PRR attempted to take part, but its desperate, last-ditch choice of joining with the New York Central provided no financial benefit, as they were parallel east-west competitors in almost identical markets, whereas the economics of successful mergers clearly favored end-to-end couplings. J. Pierpont Morgan would have been appalled at this merger. In a particularly cruel irony, the ICC approved the 1968 PRR-NYC merger only after the PRR agreed to divest itself of the Norfolk and Western, its only bankroll. Seeing the handwriting on the wall, Penn Central management attempted to diversify the company—for example, by purchasing an interest in Executive Jet Aviation and numerous real estate ventures—but it was too late.[8]

The Penn Central tipped into bankruptcy two years later, and President Nixon signed into law the Rail Passenger Service Act, creating the National Railroad Passenger Corporation, shortened to Amtrak, to be owned by the federal government. Amtrak's operations began on May 1, 1971 with a train departing New York's Penn Station for Philadelphia's 30th Street Station. Amtrak provided the passenger service, but Penn Central owned the track of the Northeast Corridor until passage of the Rail Revitalization and Regulatory Reform Act of 1976, which in addition to funding creation of Conrail, provided Amtrak with the money to acquire and upgrade the Northeast Corridor. This act also funded Amtrak's Northeast Corridor Improvement Project, which had the effect of reducing freight service on the corridor as it increased the speed of passenger trains. Conrail inherited Penn Central's Northeast Corridor freight business, but aside from servicing some auto plants on the line in North Jersey, Delaware and Maryland, it made little attempt to encourage activity. Instead, Conrail focused its management's full attention on developing east-west business, particularly the new double-stack container transport technology that revolutionized the Port of New York and New Jersey. Norfolk Southern has inherited Conrail's freight rights on the Northeast Corridor, but as of this writing, has made little if any use of them, pending completion of rate-sharing negotiations with Amtrak.

Amtrak's most popular, profitable and heavily used services are those running on the old PRR Northeast Corridor, and after the dramatic increases in gasoline prices in 2007 and 2008, Amtrak has been experiencing record ridership. But it has been clear for some time that Amtrak will never achieve a net financial break-even over its entire system and will continue to be dependent on federal operating subsidies, even after it has cut every possible cost and reformed its labor contracts to eliminate the featherbedding that characterized the Penn Central and PRR. Every year, its president plays Jonah or Daniel before Congress, pleading for Amtrak's subsidy while legislators from states with little or no Amtrak service cry foul, even as they blithely direct funds to other forms of transportation in their home districts, such as airport construction, subsidies for commuter air travel, or transfers from the General Fund to the Highway Trust Fund, amounting to $34.5 billion between 2008 and 2010. Considering the positive impact that Amtrak's services have on the northeastern United States in terms of relief from highway and air traffic corridor congestion, improved air quality and reduced dependence on foreign sources of energy with a corresponding positive impact on the balance of trade (because the Northeast Corridor runs on electricity), one might hope that Amtrak would continue to be recognized as a wise long-term investment in America.[9]

References

1. George H. Burgess and Miles C. Kennedy, *Centennial History of the Pennsylvania Railroad* (Philadelphia: The Pennsylvania Railroad, 1949) discusses the development of the Philadelphia, Wilmington and Baltimore Railroad and its acquisition by the PRR; relations with the B&O, Philadelphia Junction and Connecting Railroads, the Baltimore and Potomac Railroad; and the construction of tunnels and station to Manhattan.
2. J.V. Hare, *History of the Reading* (Philadelphia: John Henry Strock, 1966) originally appeared as articles in *The Pilot* and *Philadelphia and Reading Railway Men*, beginning in May 1909 and ending in February 1914. It gives the Reading's perspective on the

PRR's acquisition of the PW&B, the development of the Junction Railroad, relations with the B&O, and the acquisition of the North Penn and its Bound Brook Line to Newark, New Jersey.

3. Hugh R. Gibb, "Brotherly Love—Philadelphia Style," *The Bulletin of the National Railway Historical Society* (Vol. 39, No. 6, 1974) gives an account of the B&O's entry into Philadelphia; the failed attempt to acquire the Philadelphia, Wilmington and Baltimore; and problems with the PRR on the Junction and Connecting Railroads.

4. *The Encyclopedia Americana*, 1955 Edition, includes good descriptions of the PRR and the B&O, and of electric locomotives.

5. Nicholas B. Wainwright, *History of the Philadelphia Electric Company, 1881–1961* (Philadelphia: The Philadelphia Electric Company, 1961) gives a full account of the International Electric Exhibition.

6. Rudolph J. Walther, *Happenings in Ye Olde Philadelphia, 1680–1900* (Philadelphia: Walther Printing House, 1925) includes an account of the International Electric Exhibition; its use of the PRR Centennial Station; the Lehigh Avenue electric trolley; and the schedule times of P&R and PRR trains in 1874 and 1890.

7. Philadelphia City Planning Commission, *Philadelphia Railroads* (Philadelphia: PCPC Comprehensive Planning Division, 1959) discusses the cessation of the B&O's Philadelphia passenger operations and its 1956 traffic volumes.

8. Joseph R. Daughen and Peter Binzen, *The Wreck of the Penn Central* (Boston: Little, Brown, 1971; Washington, DC: Beard Books, 1999) includes a discussion of the PRR-NYC merger; the Penn Central's outside investments; and its decline and bankruptcy.

9. *Wikipedia* includes a good account of Amtrak's creation, operations and budget, and the demolition of Pennsylvania Station.

10. Thom Nickels, *Philadelphia Architecture* (Mount Pleasant, SC: Arcadia Publishing, 2005) discusses the Fairmount Water Works as America's second most popular tourist destination in the 19th century.

CHAPTER 4

Reading Terminal

sk any 10 strollers enjoying a sunny afternoon in Rittenhouse Square to name their favorite indoor public space in Philadelphia, and Reading Terminal Market is sure to get at least one mention. The railroad station that operated above the market may be a fading memory. It is unlikely to be cited even by those who can recall it. In its final days as a passenger depot, the terminal's waiting room was drab, dirty and poorly lighted, although for a rail buff, its 13-track, clear-span train shed was awesome. The market, on the other hand, has delighted the five senses of Philadelphians for generations, in fact for longer than there was a terminal, or even a railroad.

When William Penn landed in what he named Philadelphia in the autumn of 1682, he and his fellow Friends were greeted at the Blue Anchor Tavern on Dock Creek by Thomas Holmes' advance survey party and by some bemused Swedes who had settled there at least 40 years earlier and who were curious to meet their new neighbors. Soon afterward, outdoor markets consisting of crude wooden stalls sprang up on Water Street, then Philadelphia's waterfront thoroughfare. Penn had intended Water Street to be a tree-lined boulevard, but he spent little time in his colony. His wish was ignored and commerce ruled. The foot of High (Market) Street became the city's food market, with the fishmongers in the middle of High Street and the Jersey Farmers Market near the High Street wharf, where a bell was rung by fishermen bringing in catch to sell.[1]

Philadelphia grew quite rapidly, with 80 families being counted in August 1683, and 2,500 people living in 600 homes by 1685. When Penn returned to Philadelphia in 1699, it had a population of 4,500 living in 700 houses. The city had a "Noble Town House or Guild Hall, a Handsome Market House and a Convenient Prison," two warehouses, malt and brew houses, bake houses for public use, and "no beggars or old maids."[9]

In 1720, City Council resolved to erect a proper brick market on High Street, and anticipating 21st-century sensitivities, decreed that "No person be suffered to Smoak Tobacco in the Market House or in any of the Stalls." Another bell was added by the wharf to alert the market to the arrival of boats loaded with Jersey produce. In 1745, residents of the southern part of the city petitioned the Council to erect a market house on 2nd Street from Pine to Cedar (South) Streets. This market house, which survives, is a duplicate of the 1720s market, and on summer Saturdays continues to serve its purpose. Another noteworthy market of that era sprang up in 1763 on 2nd Street in Northern Liberties, extending from Hickory Lane (Fairmount Avenue) to Poplar Lane, a mirror image of the south 2nd Street market.

With the city's population growth from 41,200 in 1800 to 121,376 by 1850, the High Street outdoor food stalls grew westward, eventually extending all the way to 17th Street by 1859. By then everyone knew High Street as Market Street and in

Market shed at Front and Market Streets, successor to the market authorized by City Council in 1720. This shed was erected in 1832, but this view dates from 1859 (Courtesy of Philadelphia Industrial Development Corporation).

1853, its name was changed. Market Street had become a tangle of food stalls, dry goods stores (the forerunners of department stores), druggists, knife sharpeners, roasted chestnut vendors and string teams of horses or mules of the municipal draying cars to the Pennsylvania Railroad's freight station at 13th Street and its passenger station at 8th Street. In 1852, a movement began to abolish all the outdoor markets that were located in the beds of public streets. They were considered unsanitary and a nuisance, and a group incorporated as "The Broad Street Market House Company" erected a building on the east side of Broad Street, below Race Street, in 1854, but this venture proved to be a failure. Another market house opened on Race Street at Juniper, but it failed as well, and the city acquired it for the site of its Philadelphia Fire Department headquarters. This handsome edifice was demolished in 2008, over much protest by firemen and preservationists, to create a site for the expansion of Philadelphia's Convention Center.

In the place of these two failures, individual corporations composed mostly of farmers erected four enclosed market houses. Two of these, the Western and Eastern Markets, were later acquired and demolished for construction of the PRR's Broad

Street Station (completed 1882) and the Philadelphia Bourse (1895), but the two others, the Farmers' and the Franklin Markets, continued and prospered. The Farmers' Market was located on the north side of Market Street from 11th to 12th Streets; the Franklin Market was adjacent, on 12th Street. These two markets occupied the site coveted in 1889 by the Philadelphia and Reading Railroad for its Philadelphia terminal.[3]

That the P&R could even dream of building a new Philadelphia terminal on the scale that its management now contemplated seems unimaginable, given the incredibly turbulent times that it had just experienced, replete with bankruptcies, receiverships, reorganizations, expansions, contractions, strikes, treachery, massacre and suicide. Until 1870, the P&R had remained preoccupied with hauling large quantities of relatively low-value anthracite for relatively short distances to markets and wharves in Philadelphia and New York Harbor and keeping its British investors satisfied. But in 1870, it elected a president of outsized dreams and unbounded ambitions, a Philadelphia Napoleon named Franklin B. Gowen, who was determined to expand the P&R and challenge the PRR in every market.

Gowen was born in 1836 into a wealthy family whose home, "Magnolia Villa," was located on the grounds of what had been "Mount Airy," the colonial-era estate of Chief Justice William Allen, a portion of which today is occupied by Philadelphia's Lutheran Theological Seminary at Germantown and Gowen Avenues. The Gowen home is now the seminary's Hagan Hall. His father was an immigrant from Ulster and his mother was descended from one of Germantown's original settler families. Gowen studied law and was elected district attorney of Schuylkill County in 1862, during the rise of the Molly Maguires. These Irish immigrant miners battled the English anthracite mine owners and their Welsh and Scottish agents there and in

Farmer's Market on the north side of Market Street, east of 12th Street. This market, together with the nearby Franklin Market on North 12th Street, preceded the Reading Terminal Market. Note the boxcar on Market Street at left (Courtesy of The Library Company of Philadelphia).

Carbon County in the 1860s and early 1870s, echoing the strife that had plagued the British Isles for centuries. Gowen left public office in 1864, before the notorious trials of the Mollies had begun, and joined the Philadelphia and Reading, first heading its legal department before becoming the company's president within the short span of six years. A brilliant public speaker, dramatic stage orator and magnetic personality, Franklin Gowen quickly became the spokesman for the anthracite industry in Pennsylvania. He advanced its interests in the state legislature, suppressing miners' union organizing activity, breaking strikes and leading the efforts to arrest, convict and execute 23 Mollies in Mauch Chunk and Pottsville on the basis of evidence collected by a spy of the Pinkerton Detective Agency, which Gowen had hired. Not content with the anodyne environment of the P&R's Philadelphia headquarters on South 4th Street, he longed for a return to the courtroom limelight and did a star turn as special counsel to the prosecutor of the Mollies in 1876. Gowen was the P&R's president during the Great Railroad Strike of 1877 and the Reading Massacre on July 23rd of that year, when the state militia gunned down 11 striking P&R employees. He unsuccessfully attempted to prosecute the leadership of the striking railroad workers' union, the Brotherhood of Locomotive Engineers, again using Pinkerton spies to gather evidence.

Not content merely with hauling coal, Gowen soon doubled down the P&R's wager on the anthracite market when he created the Philadelphia and Reading Coal and Iron Company with more funds borrowed from his British investors, the House of McCalmont, to own mines and produce anthracite directly in competition with his own customers, though this was forbidden by the P&R's charter. By 1877, the price of coal had plunged because of excessive supply, and the P&R's total income barely met the interest payment to the McCalmonts on Gowen's mining investment alone. He also wanted to beat the Pennsylvania Railroad as a long-distance transporter of general freight and passengers. Swinging for the bleachers, Gowen managed to hit a home run in 1878 when he assembled a route to the Hudson River from the Philadelphia, Germantown and Norristown Railroad, the North Penn, Delaware and Bound Brook, and the Central Railroad of New Jersey, which was controlled by his friend William Vanderbilt. This accomplishment was equivalent to the PRR's coup in gaining control of the United Railroads of New Jersey seven years earlier. Gowen then built coal piers at Port Elizabeth and ran anthracite as far as Europe.

The market price of anthracite continued falling despite Gowen's efforts to manipulate its supply, and in May 1880, the Philadelphia and Reading Railroad Company and the P&R Coal and Iron Company suspended debt service payments, and the McCalmonts forced the P&R into bankruptcy. The U.S. Internal Revenue collector seized 22 of its locomotives at Port Richmond Terminal on a claim for taxes on scrip that the P&R had issued the previous year. The Philadelphia and Reading watched from the sidelines the contest of wills between the Pennsylvania

Franklin B. Gowen (1836–1889), president of the Philadelphia and Reading Railroad (1870–1884) (Courtesy of the Hagley Museum and Library, Wilmington, DE).

Railroad and the Baltimore and Ohio for control of the Philadelphia, Baltimore and Washington. In 1881, it squirmed helplessly as the PRR drove a track spike directly into the heart of the P&R's anthracite franchise by constructing its Schuylkill Valley Line from Philadelphia through Reading and Pottsville on up to New Boston Junction—101 miles of railroad within site of the P&R for almost its entire length.

In 1882, Gowen crafted a reorganization plan with the support of William Vanderbilt and Philadelphia's John Wanamaker, and launched the most controversial adventure of his entire railroad career: to extend the P&R all the way to Pittsburgh, a project that became known as the "South Penn Railroad." This was Gowen's response to the PRR Schuylkill Valley foray, and he attracted a coterie of supporters who were the face of bare-knuckle capitalism in that free-market era, including Andrew Carnegie, John D. Rockefeller, Henry Clay Frick and Chauncey Depew. But he also gained the wrath of the Pennsylvania Railroad and the unwelcome attention of the one man in the United States who at that time could be said to regulate the railroad industry's private finances—investment banker J. Pierpont Morgan. Before there was a Securities and Exchange Commission or an Interstate Commerce Commission, there was J.P. Morgan.

J. Pierpont Morgan. Before there was an Interstate Commerce Commission or a Securities and Exchange Commission, there was J.P. Morgan. In this famous photograph by Edward Steichen, Morgan wears the expression of a lion of industry with an iron will (Courtesy of the Museum of Modern Art, New York).

Chauncey Depew, president of the New York Central Railroad, had, after Gowen, the greatest reason of all the project backers for seeing the PRR humbled, as it competed head to head with his "water level route" from Albany to Buffalo along the old Erie Canal. Not to let Depew's challenge go unanswered, the PRR retaliated by buying up the stock of a New York Central competitor, the West Shore Railroad, running along the Hudson River, with the intention of diverting the NYC's traffic southward onto the PRR by cutting its freight charges. To J.P. Morgan, this rate war looked like mutually assured destruction, and as an investment banker, he foresaw only foregone dividends and bankruptcies as a result. His solution was to invite Depew and the PRR's president George Roberts for a sail on his yacht *Corsair,* and not return to harbor until an agreement had been wrung from the two presidents to terminate their projects immediately. The feckless Gowen was not invited.

Caving in to Morgan, Depew essentially sold out the South Penn Railroad, enraging its backers. An injunction to block the *Corsair* agreement was issued, but no funds were ever advanced to complete either the South Penn or West Shore projects. Gowen, isolated and marginalized, knew that his days were over at the Philadelphia and Reading, even if he could not accept that fact. Morgan won control of the P&R's Board of Managers in exchange for extending financing, forced out Gowen, and imposed an austerity regime that brought the railroad out of bankruptcy in 1888 under his acolyte, banker Austin Corbin. Corbin focused on restructuring the finances, and delegated the operation of the railroad to a rough-and-tumble Canadian, Archibald McLeod. Franklin Gowen committed suicide in 1889. An anonymous member of Morgan's syndicate prematurely composed Gowen's epitaph when interviewed by the *Philadelphia Times* newspaper on February 10, 1886:

> "In order to [reorganize the P&R] it is necessary to get rid of Mr. Gowen. We have all combined to get him out of the railroad's management, just as all the powers of Europe combined to crush Napoleon, and there will be no peace until Mr. Gowen is in St. Helena. He is an able and brilliant man and in some respects a veritable Napoleon, but he is no railroad manager. The trouble with Mr. Gowen is that he wants to be fighting all the time. When he was after the Molly Maguires he was in his element, but as a railroad manager he is a failure."

In January 1979, Governor Milton J. Shapp pardoned John J. Kehoe, convicted and hanged on evidence provided by Gowen that he was the Mollies' ringleader, on the basis of a recommendation by the Pennsylvania Parole Board after it investigated the conduct of Kehoe's trial.[4][5][6] The P&R constructed a passenger station on Gowen Avenue on land formerly part of the Gowen estate. It is logical that they would have named it after the adjacent street, like other stations on their Chestnut Hill Line, but perhaps they could not place the discredited Gowen name on any P&R property. As a result, that station is known to this day as Mount Airy Station, even though there are two other stations in the Mount Airy neighborhood. As a postscript, much of the South Penn Railroad was acquired by the Commonwealth of Pennsylvania in the early 1930s for the right-of-way of the Pennsylvania Turnpike west of Harrisburg.

It was Austin Corbin's chief operating officer, Archibald McLeod, who first had the idea to construct a magnificent new station on east Market Street, a location ideally suited to a railroad terminal for suburban and short-haul passenger trains of the type the P&R operated from its former Philadelphia, Germantown and Norristown station at nearby 9th and Green Streets. Corbin and McLeod noticed that their business model was beginning to change, with passenger and general freight traffic revenues, and even their bituminous coal revenues, growing in volume and share of the railroad's income while the anthracite market stagnated. It occurred to them that their investments should focus more on these emerging opportunities. McLeod also had contracted a serious case of edifice envy, watching the PRR erect its impressive Broad Street Station on the west side of City Hall in the early 1880s, and he determined that the Philadelphia and Reading would match it, if not outdo it. But first he had to acquire the site, and the merchants in the Farmers' and Franklin Markets were not budging.

McLeod considered using the railroad's power of condemnation to force out the merchants, but he rejected that idea as bad publicity and a cause of possible further delay if they resisted in court. After considerable negotiations, an agreement was struck whereby the P&R would pay the merchants one million dollars for their sites, keep them functioning throughout the construction process, and build them a new market beneath the terminal's train shed. The PRR tried to raise trouble but the fact that the merchants and the P&R had reached agreement, and that the resulting railroad terminal would be elevated above the grades of the city streets, made the proposed project very desirable to the mayor and City Council. On April 17, 1888, a meeting of citizens was held in the offices of the city's Board of Trade to protest the proposed erection of the elevated railroad terminal, but on April 19th, the ordinance authorizing the terminal was introduced into Select Councils, and on August 1, 1891, the city issued the permit to construct the terminal. Demolition began on April 5, 1892. For nineteenth-century Philadelphia, this was lightning speed.

The merchants got the best of all possible deals. Not only would the railroad pay them for their sites and build them a new market, but the basement of the market would be fitted with refrigerated space, and the railroad terminal above would have an elevator to move the farmers' provisions to and from the market. The relationship between railroads and provisions markets was becoming clearly beneficial to the merchant-farmers. In prior times, farmers had ridden their wagons and driven their herds to the markets, a task that required days for the trip and stays in farmers' hotels along the way. Farmers such as the Meyer Levin family of Montgomeryville, who lived near the Chestnut Hill and Spring House Turnpike, would travel this road south to Chestnut Hill and then down the Germantown and PerkiomenTurnpike to Market Street, staying along the way at such inns as the Spring House, Black Horse, Wheel Pump, White Swan and Rising Sun. The North Penn Railroad, running generally parallel to these key turnpikes, allowed the farmers to load their provisions aboard the train and arrive near or even at the market during the same day. Farmers' markets arose near railroad stations along the way, such as the rail-served Norris Street Market and ice plant in Kensington along the North Penn's yards at their American and Berks Streets passenger station, the Spring Garden Market near the P&R's station at 9th and Green Streets, and along Girard Avenue, the large Girard Avenue Market (at the 9th Street passenger station of the P&R) and the smaller Keystone Market (at 3rd and Girard on the North Penn Railroad). A truly fortunate farmer might even be able to travel into Philadelphia in the morning on the P&R, complete his business, and after a very long day, return home on the train to rest in his own bed that night and repeat the schedule starting at 4:00 a.m. the next day.[1 3 4 5 8]

Reading Terminal, located on the north side of Market Street east of 12th Street, showing the head-house and train shed completed in 1893. The offices of the *Philadelphia Inquirer* were located adjacent to the terminal before moving to the Elverson Building at Broad and Callowhill Streets (Courtesy of American Premier Underwriters, Inc.).

The desirability of having rail access to downtown markets was strong enough to motivate farmers, who were already pooling their resources to create indoor markets, to fund projects to acquire rights-of-way and to build railroad branch lines themselves, the so-called farmers' locals. As late as 1940, there were 10,000 acres of farmland within the city's boundaries, including 25 farms over 100 acres, and Northeast Philadelphia remained a prosperous agricultural area for a few years after World War II. Its farmers were among the investors in the Philadelphia and Frankford Railroad (1892–93), extended 2.6 miles from the confusingly named Frankford Junction on the Philadelphia and Reading at the Cheltenham Township border through Summerdale to the village of Frankford, and after construction, they conveyed it to the P&R to operate service to Reading Terminal. There was also a PRR farmers' local in Philadelphia, the 4.1-mile-long Bustleton Branch, built in 1870, running along the banks of the Pennypack and Wooden Bridge Creeks from

Girard Avenue Market, at 9th Street and Girard Avenue. This photo was taken in 1909, prior to the elevation of the Philadelphia and Reading Railroad's 9th Street Branch leading into Reading Terminal. Note the boxcar in the market's siding (Courtesy of PhillyHistory.org, a project of the Philadelphia Department of Records).

Holmesburg Junction on today's Northeast Corrider to a station and hotel on Welsh Road at Old Bustleton Pike.[48]

The Reading Terminal's construction was sequential, with "swing space" planned for the markets to continue to operate in the Market Street frontage—that is, the original Farmers' Market—while the Franklin Market was wrecked and the terminal train shed, designed by Wilson Brothers & Company, was constructed. After the shed and the market beneath it were completed, the merchants moved into the new market, and the P&R demolished the Market Street façade and erected its headhouse office building, designed by Francis H. Kimball: eight floors of salmon-pink brick and cream terra-cotta in Italian Renaissance style crowned with a balustrade. The first train departed the new train shed in February 1893, and not a moment too soon, as the P&R again lapsed into bankruptcy in March. In September 1897, properties of the Philadelphia and Reading Railroad and the P&R Coal and Iron Company were auctioned off in a foreclosure suit brought by the trustees of the general mortgage bonds for $20.5 million. The properties were purchased by the reorganization managers represented by J.P. Morgan & Company. When it finally

The Philadelphia and Frankford Railroad's passenger station, on the east side of Frankford Avenue north of Unity Street. The P&F, originally a farmers' local, was merged into the Reading Railroad in 1923. Passenger service to this station was discontinued shortly after the Frankford Elevated line was completed. The 2.6-mile Reading Frankford Branch was abandoned at the time that Conrail was created, April 1, 1976 (Courtesy of the Hagley Museum and Library, Wilmington, DE).

emerged from this latest collapse, P&R's finances as well as its board of managers were henceforth in the firm control of the House of Morgan, which dictated all important decisions. The City of Philadelphia was the singularly fortunate beneficiary of this major investment of P&R funds in such a magnificent terminal during the brief window of solvency and independence that the railroad enjoyed. For the city, the elevation of tracks over the local streets proved to be a gift that kept on giving, as it was not possible to just raise the tracks at the terminal's immediate approaches. Work had to be extended far back northward to the city's Piedmont elevations, relieving traffic congestion well into North Philadelphia, then a thriving neighborhood of residents working at nearby rail-served industries. The process of creating the "9th Street Viaduct" from 17th Street and Allegheny Avenue to the terminal lasted eight years until 1913, and included either new or reconstructed passenger and freight stations throughout, a particularly fine example being the five-story freight station on Spring Garden Street constructed in 1909, which since 1981 has been home to an artists' colony, the 915 Studio Building. In 1927, the Reading, as it was by now known, made the decision to electrify its Philadelphia regional commuter lines into the terminal, a process that took two years to complete.

The P&R retained its original downtown passenger station, the former Philadelphia, Germantown and Norristown terminal at 9th and Green Streets, as a freight house and repair facility until 1909, when it was demolished as the tracks in this area were elevated, and was replaced with an engine repair shop and roundhouse. The railroad demolished its passenger terminal at Broad and Callowhill Streets in 1897, as part of its project to lower the grade of its Pennsylvania Avenue Line or Subway Branch, so that the city could construct Broad Street on an overpass above the P&R tracks. In 1930, this old passenger station site was redeveloped as the Reading's Terminal Commerce Building. The North Penn Railroad station on American Street near the Norris Street Farmers' Market continued in use for some passenger service to Bethlehem into the 1920s. The author has heard stories of troop trains running on American Street from Bethlehem in World War II, the soldiers handing their letters out the windows to neighbors and passersby for mailing whenever the train stopped.[13]

The Reading Railroad watched the PRR's electrification of its Paoli and Chestnut Hill Lines with interest, but the impact of such an undertaking on the Reading's limited finances was daunting. The Reading was one of the first American buyers of diesel locomotives, with their original intention being to use them on commuter trains in order to reduce air pollution at Reading Terminal. After serious

"9th and Green," the passenger station of the Philadelphia, Germantown and Norristown Railroad. This station continued in freight service for several years after Reading Terminal opened (Courtesy of the Print and Picture Collection, Free Library of Philadelphia).

study, the railroad decided to electrify its system, beginning with its Chestnut Hill Line east of Germantown Avenue.

The Reading was able to profit from a timely coincidence while planning its electrification. As luck would have it, Philadelphia Electric Company (PECO) was at that time negotiating an interconnection with Pennsylvania Power and Light Company and Public Service Electric and Gas Company of New Jersey to transmit 220,000 volts into a PECO substation near Flat Rock Dam on the Schuylkill River. Meanwhile, PECO, having nearly completed its Conowingo Dam power-generating station on the Susquehanna River, was also exploring a route to bring into Philadelphia two additional 220,000-volt lines. PECO's president, Horace P. Liversidge, suggested combining the interconnection and the Conowingo transmission into a single substation, to be sited at the optimal location of Plymouth Meeting in Montgomery County, and coincidentally the tracks of the Reading Railroad ran nearby along the Schuylkill. Liversidge proposed that PECO negotiate an agreement with the Reading to erect transmission towers over its right-of-way, and contacted Reading's president Agnew T. Dice. Dice immediately saw the advantage of this idea, as the Reading's own power and signal lines could also be installed on these towers, saving considerable construction expense. An agreement was reached in August 1927, allowing PECO air rights occupation of the Reading from Shawmont on the Schuylkill to Westmoreland station, from where PECO's power ran in underground lines to its Hunting Park substation. The Reading's electrification program now went full throttle, and PECO's "overbuild" above the railroad tracks in the Philadelphia region has become a common sight.[7]

The Reading Terminal Market enjoyed several decades of success until the advent of supermarkets in the 1930s diminished its traffic, with A&P having the audacity to open a store on 12th Street opposite the farmers' market. Still, the Reading Terminal Market retained its reputation for freshness and quality, and as a source of rare delicacies. As for convenience, it was a common practice for orders to be phoned in to the market in the morning, with the order delivered either in the terminal's own trucks or sent out in railcars to the passenger station nearest the customer in mid-afternoon, the conductor dropping off food parcels and bundles of the *Evening Bulletin* to the stationmaster. The author remembers picking up the family order at Fern Rock Station after school in the late 1950s. The Girard Avenue and Norris Street Markets lasted into the early 1960s. The Girard Avenue Market's site on the edge of the city's Yorktown Urban Renewal Area is now a vacant lot, and one wonders if recreating a farmers' market there might still be a good alternative for maintaining the neighbors' health and well-being.

In 1963, the Philadelphia City Planning Commission released its landmark *Plan for Center City Philadelphia,* which placed a special focus on revitalizing the area east of City Hall, to complement the improvements then under way to its west, after demolition of the PRR's Broad Street Station and its elevated approach freed

The Reading's Spring Garden Street Station. Constructed in 1909, it has been an artists' colony since 1981. The lower building on the right, formerly the outbound station and platform, is on the abandoned segment of the 9th Street Branch, mentioned as a candidate for a possible Philadelphia version of New York's Highline Park (Courtesy of the Hagley Museum and Library, Wilmington, DE).

18 acres of high-value land for redevelopment as Penn Center. The improvements recommended in this 1963 plan largely define Center City's present appearance—the Market Street East retail corridor, Society Hill, Independence Mall, the Chestnut Street Transitway, and most daring of all because of its high cost and engineering design complexity, the Center City Commuter Connection Tunnel, proposed as the foundation, both economically and physically, for the Market Street East improvements. But after all, the motto of Planning Commission Executive Director Edmund Bacon was "Make no little plans." This proposed tunnel would impact decisively on the Reading Terminal, but of course it would have to await funding from a variety of sources, and the popular wisdom was that it would never be found.[10]

The project finally could be implemented in the 1970s, when funding was secured to construct the Center City Commuter Connection Tunnel linking the Reading Railroad's commuter lines, which terminated at its 12th and Market Streets train shed, and the Penn Central (formerly the PRR) commuter lines, which terminated several blocks west at Suburban Station (16th and Market Streets). Both were stub-end terminals, and linking the two would greatly improve the efficiency of both, as trains on the combined 500 route miles could then pass through from one network onto the other, enhancing rail commuting as far afield as Trenton, Downingtown, Doylestown and Wilmington, and increasing the value of sites near the two downtown stations and 30th Street Station in nearby West Philadelphia. The funding, delivered during the waning days of the Ford Administration by Secretary of Transportation William Coleman, a Philadelphian, allowed the city to implement the dream of Market Street East as envisioned by the Planning Commission. Philadelphians occasionally prove correct the adage of Claire Booth Luce that no good deed goes unpunished. This was on display when Secretary Coleman made his announcement, and the media and the public pounced, proclaiming the "absurdity" of spending $330 million to benefit suburban commuters when the funds should have been spent on helping city residents. One wag said that the tunnel would benefit only those three attorneys who lived in Doylestown and practiced in Media. Even Mayor Frank Rizzo was initially cool, preferring that his priority transportation project, the Airport High-Speed Rail Line, take precedence, but farsighted civic leadership and construction trade union lobbying prevailed and the funds were accepted.

Completed in 1985, the 1.3-mile-long tunnel is a masterpiece of engineering, requiring the four tracks to pass over the Broad Street Subway, with the tunnel's roof just two feet beneath the roadway surface of John F. Kennedy Boulevard, to pass under Philadelphia's 1927-era City Hall Annex, which required extensive underpinning, around the foundations of the historic Masonic Temple and through those of the Reading Terminal and Suburban Station. According to its project manager, Urban Engineers' Joseph P. McAtee, "The project brought hundreds of engineers in the design and construction professions together in one of the best demonstrations of teamwork Philadelphia has ever seen." "It was the tunnel nobody wanted, a tunnel that threatened to go nowhere, whose railroads it connects went bankrupt," reported the American Society of Civil Engineers in awarding the project its 1985 Outstanding Civil Engineering Achievement citation.[11]

The tunnel was constructed to allow for "overbuild" of future buildings atop it, and the first of these was the Gallery, a multilevel shopping center and department store connected to the commuter and subway networks. It occupied a central location along Market Street above the tunnel's commuter rail station at 11th and Market Streets and adjacent to Reading Terminal Market. In the early 1980s, the decision was made to construct a new convention center in Philadelphia, and in a contest of alternative locations the Reading Company's proposal of their terminal won out over master builder John McShain's proposed site at 17th and Vine Streets. The Reading Terminal Market managed to survive through the disruptions and dislocations of the convention center's construction activity and the environmental remediation of the train shed above it just as its predecessors, the Farmers' and Franklin Markets, had weathered the early 1890s. They now emerged with a newfound addition to their customer base—conventioneers. The Convention Center incorporated the Reading's train shed, placed on the National Register of Historic Places in 1972 and declared a National Historic Landmark in 1976, as a foyer to its main exhibition space. This decision retained the grandeur of the shed's single-span arched roof and restored the beautiful Italianate façade of the Reading's headhouse as a grand entrance where the Convention Center's offices and smaller meeting rooms are also located. An infusion of new Reading Terminal Market tenants and an expansion of dining and entertainment space have retained the market's reputation as one of Philadelphians' favorite places.

Ironically, the project had an unintended consequence—the breaking of the "gentlemen's agreement" in Philadelphia that no building should exceed the height of the hat on the statue of William Penn atop City Hall at Centre Square, as nearby sites were now too valuable to be limited by that unwritten proscription. This "rule" was dear to the heart of Edmund Bacon, who had also led the effort to preserve the train shed during the Reading's darkest days, but by now this limitation had given the downtown a "crew cut" appearance that was, by 1987's opening of the soaring Liberty Place office building, mercifully out of fashion. Bacon's support for one of his favorite projects had unwittingly led to the undoing of another. Office, residential and hotel development projects since then, such as the Cira Center at 30th Street Station and the Comcast Center near Suburban Station, have given Philadelphia an eclectic, modern skyline, thanks to the tunnel project making the downtown and West Philadelphia more convenient commutes, and it filled Reading Terminal Market with customers.[12]

With the tunnel's completion, the rail line elevated in the late 19th century into Reading Terminal was abandoned as far north as Poplar Street. Demolition being too expensive, this structure has remained untouched, ignored and unwanted for almost three decades. But recently, plans have been floated to convert it to an above-grade park similar to Manhattan's High Line, an abandoned railroad overpass that has quickly become a unique recreational amenity for the revitalized nearby Chelsea Piers and Meat Packing neighborhoods. If this conversion occurs, perhaps renovation of the abandoned Reading Spring Garden Station, across from the 915 Studio Building artists' colony, can revive yet another charming relic of Philadelphia's rich railroad past.

References

1. Rudolph J. Walther, *Happenings in Ye Olde Philadelphia, 1680–1900* (Philadelphia: Walther Printing House, 1925), gives accounts of early farmers' markets, fish markets, Camptown and Fishtown, and the Reading Terminal's ordinance, demolition, site work and construction.

2. *The Port of Philadelphia: Its History, Facilities and Advantages, Department of Wharves, Docks and Ferries* (City of Philadelphia, 1926), discusses the early waterfront, Water Street and the early markets.

3. David K. O'Neil, *Reading Terminal Market: An Illustrated History* (Philadelphia: Camino Books, 2004), gives an account of the Reading Terminal Market's operations to the present time.

4. Jay V. Hare, *History of the Reading: Collected Articles by Mr. Jay V. Hare* (Philadelphia: John Henry Strock, 1926), discusses the history of the Philadelphia and Reading Railroad and the construction of the Reading Terminal.

5. James L. Holton, *The Reading Railroad: History of a Coal Age Empire,* Vols. 1 and 2 (Laury's Station, PA: Garrigues House, Publishers, 1989), gives an account of Philadelphia and Reading Railroad operations and financial difficulties; the regimes of Gowan, Corbin and McLeod; and the influence of J.P. Morgan.

6. George H. Burgess and Miles C. Kennedy, *Centennial History of the Pennsylvania Railroad, 1846–1946* (Philadelphia: The Pennsylvania Railroad, 1949), gives the Pennsylvania Railroad's version of the South Penn Railroad and the construction of the Schuylkill Valley Railroad.

7. Nicholas B. Wainwright, *History of the Philadelphia Electric Company, 1881–1961* (Philadelphia: The Philadelphia Electric Company, 1961), gives the story of the Reading Railroad's electrification.

8. Frederic M. Miller, Morris J. Vogel and Allen E. Davis, *Still Philadelphia: A Photographic History, 1890–1940* (Philadelphia: Temple University Press, 1983), discusses agricultural acreage in Philadelphia in 1940.

9. *Encyclopedia Americana* (1955 Edition) gives a full description of life in colonial Philadelphia.

10. Philadelphia City Planning Commission, *The Plan for Center City Philadelphia* (Philadelphia: PCPC, 1963), discusses the conceptual origins of the Center City Commuter Connection Tunnel.

11. Urban Engineers, "Over, Under, Around and Through" (Philadelphia: Urban Engineers, 50th Anniversary Celebration press release, 2010), gives an account of the planning and construction of the Center City Commuter Connection Tunnel.

12. Urban Engineers, "Changing the Skyline, and Rarely Seeing the Light of Day" (Philadelphia: Urban Engineers, 50th Anniversary press release, 2010), discusses the revitalization of Center City Philadelphia resulting from the construction of the CCCC Tunnel.

13. Peg McLaughlin, oral account of World War II troop trains on American Street's North Penn Railroad.

14. Joseph F. Folk, *The Philadelphia Terminal: A Description of Penn Central's Freight Operations in a Major Urban Terminal* (Philadelphia: The Penn Central Company, 1973), gives a history of the Bustleton Branch.

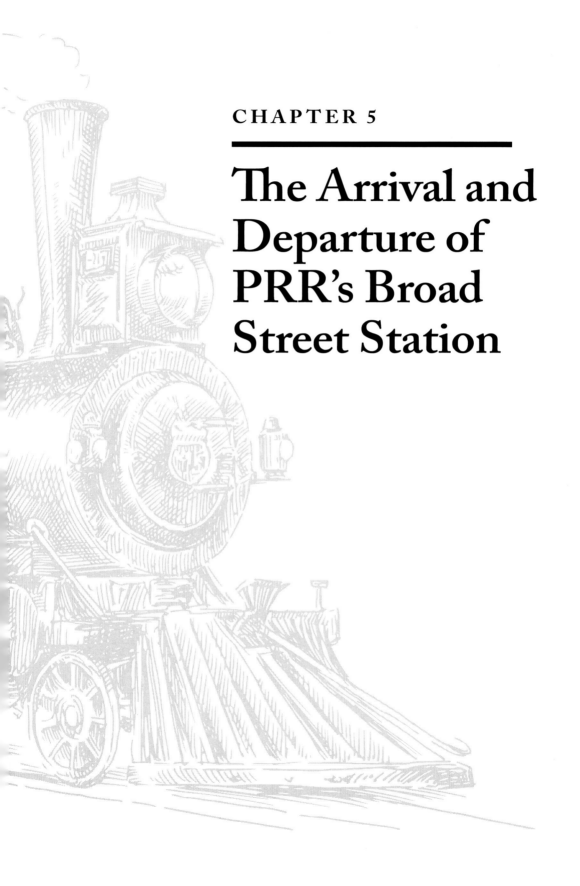

CHAPTER 5

The Arrival and Departure of PRR's Broad Street Station

ycling south along the path of Schuylkill River Park, below the Philadelphia Museum of Art, riders see to their left what could be mistaken for an obelisk standing adjacent to the CSX railroad tracks. Looking across the tracks, they see the obelisk's companion and recognize that the pair of structures must be piers that once supported something. These two structures are some of the very few physical remains of what once was Philadelphia's grand railroad station in its gilded era, the Pennsylvania Railroad's Broad Street Station. These structures once supported the trestle carrying one of the station's approach tracks over the Schuylkill River.

By 1870, its Connecting and Junction Railroads had freed the PRR from dependency on the horse- and mule-drawn municipal string-team system operating on downtown Philadelphia streets, allowing it all-locomotive access to its other two stations in Philadelphia County—the former Philadelphia, Wilmington and Baltimore station at Broad and Prime (now Washington Avenue) Streets, and the former Philadelphia and Trenton Railroad's Kensington Depot at Front and Berks Streets. The PRR had artfully withdrawn from but encircled the congested central city, and in 1876, it had built its new Centennial Station at 32nd and Market Streets in West Philadelphia, from which the railroad could efficiently handle passenger trains either passing through Philadelphia or terminating there. But within five years, the PRR would recross the Schuylkill and occupy its colossal new Broad Street Station across 15th Street from City Hall on Centre Square. For the next 72 years, it would confront the challenges of operating a stub-end terminal serving both through and terminating traffic. How it addressed these challenges would have an indelible impact on the Philadelphia region's transportation system and the city's physical form.

The PRR's Connecting Railroad project included a station in West Philadelphia built in 1864 at 30th and Market Streets. The end of the Civil War brought only a brief drop in passenger traffic while freight loadings held steady, and soon passenger volumes rebounded. As Philadelphia and the nation prepared to celebrate the 100th anniversary of the Declaration of Independence in 1876, the Pennsylvania Railroad decided to replace its 30th Street Station with a new one, Centennial Station, the most elaborate that the PRR had yet built. It was located at the northwest corner of 32nd and Market Streets in West Philadelphia, with a loop track connecting it to the PRR satellite Fairgrounds Station at the city's Centennial Exhibition site at Belmont and Parkside Avenues. PRR preparations for the 1876 Centennial celebration included four-tracking its West Philadelphia approaches and refurnishing its passenger cars in anticipation of the large number of expected attendees. Visitors would not only tour the exhibition, but take home and share their opinions of the railroad, and management was not about to waste this public relations opportunity. The Centennial was judged a major success, with over 9.9 million people visiting between its May 10th opening and its November 10th closing—a triumph for its planners and the Pennsylvania Railroad.

The Pennsylvania Railroad's Centennial Station. It was built in 1876 at 32nd and Market Streets, site of the Franklin Institute's 1884 International Electrical Exhibition (Courtesy of the Germantown Historical Society, Philadelphia, PA).

Shortly after the Centennial closed, PRR's management began considering alternative routes to reach the anthracite regions of Pennsylvania then dominated by the rival Philadelphia and Reading Railroad. One possibility studied consisted of a new line extending northward from the just-completed Connecting Railroad in the general vicinity of North Broad Street through Germantown, Chestnut Hill, Conshohocken and Norristown to the city of Bethlehem in the Lehigh Valley, where Josiah White had started mining coal 50 years earlier. This route would generally parallel the North Pennsylvania Railroad that the P&R had recently acquired. Management rejected this alternative as too costly, deciding instead to construct their Schuylkill Valley Line, but they opted to build only a short portion of the Germantown Line, as far as Chestnut Hill, primarily for commuter service. This was the brainchild of PRR director Henry H. Houston, who coincidentally owned hundreds of acres of land within walking distance of the proposed line, and who, from his Chestnut Hill estate "Drum Moir" ("great house" in Gaelic), oversaw development of much of Northwest Philadelphia. The point where this line met the Connecting Railroad a short distance west of Broad Street became known as Germantown Junction, the site of a railroad station that eventually grew into North Philadelphia Station, 30 blocks north of City Hall. Planning for this line, and then for this station, coincided with PRR management's deliberations on creating a new station in Philadelphia's central business district.[7]

The impetus for a downtown station east of the Schuylkill River must have come from the public and the politicians, who regarded the 32nd and Market Street station as too remote from the city's center, and clamored for redress. It certainly could not have come from the PRR's operating department, which must have hated the idea. While serving the old PRR passenger stations along Market Street consecutively at 18th, 8th, 11th and 13th Streets had been an operating nightmare, these stations were convenient for the passengers who used them, most of whom worked and resided nearby. Colonel Thomas A. Scott (1823–1881), the PRR's president from 1874 to 1880, started planning for an elevated train line in 1879. He needed a grade-separated, stub-end station next to the site of City Hall at Centre

The Pennsylvania Railroad's Broad Street Station (1881–1952), designed by Frank Furness (Courtesy of The Library Company of Philadelphia).

Square. The station and its approach tracks would occupy an entire city block in width between Market and Filbert Streets. The tracks would be supported on fill between masonry retaining walls, and the numbered north-south streets would pass under them in block-long tunnels. To Philadelphians, this half-mile approach looked like the Great Wall of China, hence its nickname, "The Chinese Wall." A new bridge across the Schuylkill River to the PRR's 30th Street yards was also deemed necessary. The railroad began buying the properties within the 18 acres needed for this venture, including the West Market, the farmers' market serving Center City west of Centre Square.

Construction was sequential, with the train shed, designed by Wilson Brothers & Company, completed and opened for operation on December 5, 1881. The headhouse, elaborate as a mad Bavarian's castle, was designed by noted Philadelphia architect Frank Furness. It opened in 1893, housing waiting rooms and the PRR's corporate headquarters. Wilson Brothers would go on to design the P&R's Reading Terminal train shed several blocks east, and would enlarge the PRR Broad Street Station train shed several times. Furness would design many other railroad stations in the Middle Atlantic area.

Broad Street Station's approaches for north-south intercity traffic were designed as a "Y," with the intercity train leaving the main line, crossing the Schuylkill River, heading into the stub-end station, loading and discharging passengers, and then backing out again, crossing the Schuylkill onto the main track to continue its route. This complicated maneuver added up to a half-hour delay onto the intercity train's schedule. Traffic volumes grew with the general prosperity of the decades following its opening, and soon the PRR was handling over 500 trains each weekday into and out of Broad Street Station. Of these, 40 percent were through trains and the remainder were commuter trains to central Philadelphia from throughout the region. Anyone who has visited a tourist railway and seen the exhaust smoke emitting from just one steam locomotive can begin to imagine the air quality resulting from 500 of them at Broad Street Station, and not more than six blocks eastward, hundreds more puffing away at Reading Terminal. When shady deals were cut in City Hall's smoke-filled back rooms, tobacco fumes weren't the only pollutants.[16]

The Pennsylvania Railroad's success in electrifying its operations in New York City, and its experiences with electric operations on the Long Island Rail Road, in which it had acquired a controlling interest in 1900, caused it to consider electrifying its Philadelphia commuter operations in order to reduce air and noise pollution. It also observed the local experience of the Philadelphia Rapid Transit Company, which electrified its suburban lines to Media and Chester, purchasing electricity from the newly formed Philadelphia Electric Company. In June 1913, the railroad entered into negotiations with PECO for power to be supplied to its commuter lines from Broad Street Station to Paoli and Chestnut Hill. The PRR had the option either to purchase its electricity or to generate it on its own, as other railroads were now doing, and chose the former alternative, deciding to purchase a single-phase, 11,000-volt alternating service. This was a new type of service that could not be supplied by PECO's three-phase generators, and engineers struggled for over a year to devise a means to spread the single-phase load automatically and equally on all three phases. This service was so radically different that General Electric Company designed and built two complicated phase-balancers and shipped them to Philadelphia without testing them. But when they were installed at PECO's Schuylkill Station, they operated perfectly. For economy and dependability, the wisdom of the decision by Gibbs and Hill, Inc., the PRR's consultant electrical engineers, to opt for single-phase service resulted in PECO's assuming the largest railroad electrification load in the world.

Construction of the electrical power distribution system began on the Paoli Line in late 1913 and on the Chestnut Hill Line in 1915, with electrified train service beginning there in April 1918. Grade crossing elimination work coincided with the electrical work. PECO supplied power to feed these two lines from its Schuylkill station to a railroad substation at the PRR's Arsenal Bridge, so named for its proximity to the federal Schuylkill Arsenal near Grays Ferry.[2] Electrification of these two lines relieved congestion somewhat at Broad Street Station, but only to a minor degree, as traffic growth on all passenger lines continued unabated.

The burdensome schedule penalty extracted by the "Y" maneuver led to the PRR designating a new station in North Philadelphia, built on the Connecting Railroad in 1901 near North Broad Street and Germantown Junction, as the Philadelphia station for through passenger trains operating between New York and Harrisburg (and all other points west). North Philadelphia Station was the sole Philadelphia stop for the *Broadway Limited* ("The Aristocrat of the Rails"), *The American* ("Worthy of the Name it Bears") and other PRR express New York trains that made the North Philadelphia–Penn Station run in an hour and 45 minutes. These trains would enter the Connecting Railroad at Zoo (or Mantua) Junction to and from the west and would no longer travel southward into Broad Street Station. The PRR then used its new West Philadelphia Station (at 32nd and Market Streets), constructed in 1903, to service Philadelphia passengers on its New York-to-Washington trains, which could then avoid Broad Street Station. North Philadelphia Station, a gray limestone and terra-cotta structure in Italian Renaissance and French Chateau style designed by Theophilus Parsons Chandler Jr., founder of the University of Pennsylvania's Department of Architecture, is listed on the National Register of Historic Places.[10]

In the middle of all this passenger train activity at the "Y," freight trains still rumbled through the 30th Street yards, either to and from points north, south or west of the city or the piers in South Philadelphia. In 1904, the PRR constructed a three-mile-long, elevated, double-tracked trestle above these yards, stretching from

The Pennsylvania Railroad's North Philadelphia Station, built in 1901 near Germantown Junction on the Connecting Railroad. The station was designed by Theophilus Parsons Chandler, Jr. (Courtesy of The Library Company of Philadelphia).

the Junction Railroad in Grays Ferry to the Connecting Railroad in Mantua as a freight bypass to try to relieve this additional traffic burden. Clearly, no matter what improvements the PRR could make to its approaches, Broad Street Station had become an operational nightmare.

Adding to the PRR's woes, the City of Philadelphia had initiated planning for a grand parkway extending on a diagonal from Centre Square northwestward to the former city reservoir at Fairmount, where a new municipal art museum was proposed. The Benjamin Franklin Parkway, placed on the City Plan in 1903, would conflict with any future expansion of Broad Street Station, and the parkway's advocates and many other Philadelphians were increasingly vocal in their dislike of the station's "Chinese Wall" approach, with its block-long tunnels for north-south streets blighting the neighborhoods to its north. The city's concurrent plans to extend East River Drive southward to below Locust Street and to erect a municipal convention hall at 24th and Market Streets further complicated PRR expansion possibilities.

Inspired by the Columbian Exhibition of 1893 in Chicago, the parkway concept was nurtured during a period of revived civic beautification through classicism, a movement known to its advocates as "The City Beautiful," with an emphasis placed on clean, uncluttered geometry. This movement struck an immediate chord in Philadelphia, whose Fairmount Water Works design reflected Roman temple neoclassicism, and which was located within site of the proposed parkway. Demolition for the Benjamin Franklin Parkway began in 1907, when the first brick was knocked off a chimney at 422 North 22nd Street, and 11 and a half years later the boulevard was completed, implementing the 1917 final parkway plan of Parisian architect Jacques Gréber. Noted architects practicing in Philadelphia worked on the design of buildings and streets along the great thoroughfare: Horace Trumbauer and Julian Abele's 1919 Philadelphia Museum of Art and 1927 Philadelphia Free Library; sculptor Alexander Calder's 1924 Swann Memorial Fountain in Logan Circle, designed by Wilson, Eyre and McIlvaine; and Jacques Gréber and Paul Phillipe Cret's 1929 Rodin Museum. The project captured the imaginations of city residents, who now began to see PRR's Broad Street Station with its grandiose Victorian style as a blight on their civic improvement. In comparison to the restrained neoclassical parkway, this overwrought Gothic pile of brick, terra-cotta and granite seemed to strike a discordant note of eccentricity, like an uncle arriving drunk at a christening. The parkway improvement may have been the final impetus that convinced the Pennsylvania Railroad that Broad Street Station's days were numbered.[6][9][11]

Broad Street Station also had a major impact on the neighborhood to its south, Rittenhouse Square, although less immediately apparent than on the proposed parkway corridor. Philadelphia's development had proceeded from the Delaware River docks westward, and until the relocation of City Hall to Centre Square, its office core of custom house brokers, ships' agents, banks, and law and accounting firms had clustered around Independence Hall and Washington Square, while the western area toward Rittenhouse Square was decidedly more residential. With construction beginning on the new City Hall in 1871 and on Broad Street Station in 1880, this office core shifted westward. A glimpse of what downtown Philadelphia must have been like in the 1870s, before this shift began, can be found in the autobiography of Senator George Wharton Pepper (1867–1961), published in 1944. Senator Pepper recounted that as a boy growing up at 346 South 16th Street, near Rittenhouse Square, his playground was the street, but he and his friends were little disturbed by carts and carriages that passed now and then or by the occasional horse-drawn trolley. The site of his church, Saint Mark's, at 16th and Locust Streets, had the charm of the frontier, with nothing much west of it but great open spaces, and it seemed to him that his neighborhood was a village.[5] Broad Street Station was one of Philadelphia's first high-rise office buildings, employing an internal steel frame for load-bearing rather than relying on the load capacity of its exterior walls, as in the case of City Hall. This concentration of employment and economic activity in a high-rise structure on such a relatively small footprint generated concentric rings of rising property values as commercial development gravitated around it. Soon the old mansions of Walnut Street and the Sunday afternoon promenades of fashionably dressed churchgoers after services to Rittenhouse Square gave way to office buildings, shops, hotels and apartment houses. George Pepper's village had become the city.

In 1923, the Pennsylvania Railroad began serious planning for the replacement of Broad Street Station. Its experience with its electrified suburban routes led the PRR to believe that this suburban function could still be accommodated in the vicinity of Broad Street Station, but underground beneath an office building, where it would create no conflicts with the city's traffic or its parkway design. As for the intercity service, which the PRR was already trying to segregate as much as possible on the Schuylkill's west bank, the railroad proposed a station in the modern neoclassical style, on a scale with its facilities in New York, that would declare its commitment to its home city. This facility, to be located at the site of the 1864 station at 30th Street, would be on two levels: a lower level for the intercity traffic, and an upper one for suburban traffic crossing overhead at 90 degrees to the lower tracks and the Schuylkill River on its approach to the suburban station. There would be no "Sesquicentennial Station" ready in time for the 1926 festivities, but the PRR wasted no time in publicizing its plans. The celebration's official auto guide, published in 1925, prematurely proclaimed that "a magnificent new station in West Philadelphia at the Schuylkill River is planned and under construction."[6][8]

Once the two new stations—Suburban and 30th Street—had been completed, then the sites of Broad Street Station and its approach tracks, covering 18 acres, could be developed with new office buildings staffed by workers commuting to their jobs on the PRR. But first, there were municipal improvements that the railroad and the city agreed needed to be completed, notably relocation of the Market-Frankford Elevated into a tunnel, and then completion of Suburban Station. This occurred on schedule in 1930, but completion of 30th Street Station was delayed by the Depression and World War II as well as by the city lagging behind in upholding its end of the agreement. All of these projects needed to be completed before Broad Street Station could be razed and the value of its cleared site begun to be realized. The great station remained in service until April 27, 1952, the last train departing to the strains of the Philadelphia Orchestra playing Auld Lang Syne.

It is not widely known that during the 20th century there were two Broad Street Stations in Philadelphia, and that one of them still exists. The Pennsylvania Railroad was not the only provider of intercity passenger service in Philadelphia, finding itself in competition with the rival Baltimore and Ohio, which endeavored to provide a regular first-class alternative between New York and Washington, D.C. This was accomplished with its "Royal Blue Line" service, running from December 15, 1886 until April 27, 1958, when its last scheduled passenger train from Philadelphia left the station at 8:32 p.m., without orchestral accompaniment.

The Royal Blue Line traveled over B&O's tracks from Washington to its Philadelphia station at 24th and Chestnut Streets, and for its northward leg, it interchanged onto the Reading at Park Junction in Fairmount, near the Philadelphia Museum of Art. Here it could, and occasionally did, follow the "Subway Branch" (see Chapter 1) into Reading Terminal, or else continue directly northward to a stop at Wayne Junction Station and thence onto the Reading's Philadelphia, Germantown and Norristown, North Penn, and Delaware and Bound Brook lines to the Central Railroad of New Jersey, finally arriving at its terminus in Jersey City. The fact that it did not go all the way into Manhattan was a major shortcoming that the B&O sought to overcome with superior equipment and dining service, but because of station locations and service frequency, the PRR was far more popular than the B&O in ambience.

The PRR's announcement that it would replace Broad Street Station and electrify its Philadelphia-Wilmington route galvanized the B&O into action. First it produced fanciful concept drawings of a massive new station for the site of its existing one, taking into account the city's proposal to extend East River Drive southward past this location as part of its parkway project. Then, observing how well the PRR's North Philadelphia Station relieved its downtown Philadelphia congestion problems for its premium passenger services, the B&O, by now in control of the Reading, arranged for the Reading to announce in 1928 that it, too, had its own grandiose terminal construction project planned. North Broad Street Station would replace a smaller, unassuming commuter stop at Huntington Street, several blocks south of the PRR's North Philadelphia Station. The neoclassical Reading station, designed by Horace Trumbauer and Julian Abele of buff-colored Indiana limestone on a granite base with a colonnade of 12 Ionic columns facing Broad Street, had an enormous and lavish waiting room and a platform length for a dozen

The Reading's North Broad Street Station. Designed by Horace Trumbauer and Julian Abele, it was completed in 1930 (Courtesy of the Hagley Museum and Library, Wilmington, DE).

Trackside elevation of the North Broad Street Station (Courtesy of The Library Company of Philadelphia).

railcars. Far too elaborate a transportation temple for the light commuter traffic at Huntington Street, it was really intended to be the B&O's Philadelphia stop on the Reading for its Royal Blue Line, preferred as an alternative to the railroad's existing station, a Victorian-era Furness design by then as much out of fashion as the PRR's Broad Street Station. Built at a cost of two million dollars, this Reading North Broad Street Station, dedicated on September 28, 1929, opened with fanfare in 1930.[10] [12]

Alas, the fickle B&O changed its plans, perhaps because the economic turndown that coincided with the new station's construction turned into the Great Depression. So it continued running the Royal Blue Line through Wayne Junction Station, leaving North Broad Street Station to be a perennial white elephant. The station building, but not the station platform, was finally sold in 1960 for a small fraction of its construction cost. In the 1970s, the station building was converted into the Inn Towner Motor Hotel and became a focal point for a community-originated, African-American–themed Bicentennial celebration called Blaxpo. Today it is home to social agencies serving the neighborhood around it.

Time has not improved either North Broad Street Station or Wayne Junction Station. The baseball stadium opposite North Broad Street Station, known as the Baker Bowl, home to the National League Phillies and the site of Babe Ruth's last professional baseball game, was demolished in 1950. Industries that had clustered along the rail lines running past both stations relocated or went out of business. This was a citywide trend that had begun as early as Baldwin's move from Bush Hill to Eddystone, but it accelerated after World War II as the city's rising business tax burden, its reputation for aggressive union organizing of local manufacturers, and the functional obsolescence of its multi-story factory loft buildings drove businesses away.

Interior of the North Broad Street Station (Courtesy of The Library Company of Philadelphia).

John Evans Sons is a representative example of this trend. "America's Oldest Springmaker," founded by a Welsh immigrant blacksmith in New Haven, Connecticut in 1850, had moved to the "Workshop of the World" in 1870 on the advice of Evans' customers that a Philadelphia presence during the Centennial Exhibition would be advantageous for his growing business. After 97 years in Bush Hill, this firm opted to move to its present location 20 miles north in Lansdale, one of 153 manufacturing businesses to depart Philadelphia in 1967. John Evans Sons was typical of Philadelphia manufacturers, which averaged 67 employees and, unlike in other cities dependent on a single industry like steel or autos, were distributed among a wide variety of industries ranging from apparel to lumber and wood products. In 1967, John Evans Sons was just one of 430 Philadelphia firms fabricating metal products, but one of 19 of them to leave the city that year.[15] [16] [17]

By 1967, Philadelphia's industrial base was already eroding, and losses would accelerate in the coming decades as manufacturing employment declined from 246,300 in 1967 to 68,500 in 1990 and to 23,600 by 2011. Regardless of the local causes for its decline, Philadelphia had become a harbinger for manufacturing activity and employment trends across the entire nation, from Pittsburgh in the '80s to Detroit in 2007, as firms sought out new manufacturing locales with the lowest possible labor costs and taxes and the highest productivity. [15] [16]

The Reading's Wayne Junction Station continued through this period to serve its vital role as the center of the Reading's commuter rail operations, with lines radiating from it in all directions, but its ridership declined apace with its physical condition as it became a station to be endured rather than enjoyed. Reading soldiered on with its Reading Terminal-to-Newark passenger service, operating its *Crusader* and *Wall Street* Budd diesel-electric trains daily. North Broad Street Station and Wayne Junction Station continued as Philadelphia stops until the advent of Conrail, which converted its route to high-speed freight operations. Fortunately, Wayne Junction Station's current owner, Southeastern Pennsylvania Transportation Authority (SEPTA), recently announced that it has secured funds to rehabilitate this once-grand structure, building on its excellent transportation connections in order to foster transit-oriented development of the large vacant sites around it. One hopes that North Broad Street Station will someday be the focus of similar optimism. [13]

The Reading's Wayne Junction Station (Courtesy of the Hagley Museum and Library, Wilmington, DE).

The demolition of the PRR's Broad Street Station allowed one of Philadelphia's largest development projects ever, Penn Center, to proceed in the middle to late 1950s, mainly on the site formerly occupied by the Chinese Wall. Narrow Filbert Street was widened to create a grand boulevard extending from City Hall to the Schuylkill, providing a gateway and a dramatic vista to the planned 30th Street Station—or, as the PRR formally named it, Pennsylvania Station at 30th Street. Originally Pennsylvania (now JFK) Boulevard, it became lined with office and apartment buildings, with walkways at and below ground level—the Penn Center Concourse. New office buildings lined West Market Street, including the PRR's new headquarters at 6 Penn Center. The project gave new life to downtown Philadelphia, extending its attractiveness as a center of office activity for another three decades until a new round of development occurred in the 1980s, beginning in 1984, when Willard G. Rouse 3rd broke ground for Liberty Place.

In January 1988, the Philadelphia City Planning Commission issued its *Plan for Center City,* prompted six years earlier by Willard Rouse's stated intention to construct Liberty Place to a height greater than the top of the statue of William Penn cresting City Hall. This was a master stroke by Rouse, bold beyond many Philadelphians' imaginations, that set the Quaker City's traditional movers and

Remnant of Broad Street Station: a pier and abutment of the "Y" track (Author's photo).

shakers aquiver and afforded the Planning Commission an opportunity to articulate a vision of what Philadelphia could look like and be like in the year 2000. Its plan divided Center City into five districts for analysis and recommendations, and one of these—the Market West District—overlapped to a considerable degree the 1950s Penn Center, at least for its analysis of trends in office space development and employment. The Planning Commission found that this district accounted for 40 percent of Philadelphia's downtown office space, one third (or 85,000) of its workers, and the highest concentration of white-collar employees in the region. It seized on the district's transportation amenities developed by the PRR (or, in the case of the subway station and concourse, because of the PRR) as the basis for many of its recommendations for continued growth and improvement. Fortunately, many of the improvements that this 1988 Market West District Plan recommended have been implemented, although they are too numerous to list here.

Demolition of Broad Street Station was completed by McCloskey & Company in 1953, and unlike the complainants' chorus that accompanied the end of Penn Station, there were no recriminations. If Penn Station ended up in the Meadowlands, where lay Broad Street Station's remains? The Hagley Museum's PRR Chronology for March 19, 1954 states that rubble from the station and the Chinese Wall was used as fill under Greenwich Pier 122 and its railyard, and indeed the stevedore of Pier 122 has reported seeing what appeared to be bits of cornices along the shoreline after heavy storms. The PRR's choice of March 19th, the feast day of Saint Joseph, to announce that they had buried their old station under their new pier no doubt gave the devout Catholic Matt McCloskey a good laugh. Maybe he suggested it.

The PRR Chronology does not state that all of the fill was used at Pier 122, and clues occasionally turn up that some of it may have found its way onto additional sites nearby. Until after World War II, South Philadelphia east of 26th Street and below Oregon Avenue, except for the Sesquicentennial fairgrounds and the railroad

The "Spirit of Transportation" bas-relief plaque, transferred from Broad Street Station to 30th Street Station (From the author's collection).

and military facilities, was an area composed mainly of small farms, marshes and shanties, known as "The Neck." This was linked to the rest of the city before Broad Street was extended there by an ancient, meandering farm road, Stonehouse Lane, which ended at the Greenwich Point ferry to Gloucester City, New Jersey. Old-time South Philadelphians like "Big Bob" DeMento from Schnell Street near the Italian Market tell stories of going hunting down in The Neck. The way they describe it, The Neck must have been a rather rugged, unregulated place, its remoteness from Center City measured in more ways than just distance. The city burned trash for decades on an open lot near the "Sesqui's" Municipal (later JFK) Stadium, until constructing a proper incinerator in 1951. As late as the 1950 Census, fewer than 400 people lived there east of Broad Street, and 90 percent of them lacked indoor plumbing.[14] Long before, The Neck had been farmed by Stephen Girard, whose country estate "Gentilhommiere" was nearby in what is now the fashionable Girard Estate neighborhood. In addition to his many talents and interests, Girard was an epicure who introduced America to such French delicacies as broccoli and cauliflower, which he grew on his farm. Below The Neck was an open channel of water linking the Delaware and Schuylkill Rivers, and below that channel, League Island was developed as the Philadelphia Navy Base, beginning in the mid-1870s.

The channel of water was gradually filled in from the 1880s to the 1950s, first with dredge material from removal of Smith's and Windmill Islands in the Delaware River, and later by the activities of the Army Corps of Engineers in maintaining and improving the Delaware's depth. This man-made land became the site of the Greenwich Rail Yard, by the end of World War II the PRR's principal freight terminal in Philadelphia. North of Greenwich Yard and east of Broad Street, the city created the Philadelphia Food Distribution Center (FDC) in 1955, a 400-acre area of land where Girard once grew his vegetables. Occasionally, construction projects in and around the FDC, most recently the Samuels & Son seafood processing facility, unearth large, long-buried chunks of masonry debris. Perhaps therein lie some more of the remains of the PRR's Broad Street Station.

An intriguing question is why Broad Street Station was ever built, as it should have been recognized during its planning stage as an obvious step backward and an operational nightmare waiting to happen. The answer may lie in the personalities of those who struggled to grasp control of the Pennsylvania Railroad in the decades after the Civil War. J. Edgar Thomson is regarded as the PRR's finest president, expanding the railroad to conform to the contours that generally characterized it as late as its merger with the New York Central in 1968. Thomson was not just an accomplished executive, he was a highly competent engineer, trained in the United States and Britain, who had a great deal of varied railroad development experience even before becoming a PRR employee. He died on the job in 1874 without appointing an heir apparent, and a power struggle ensued involving the PRR's Senior Vice President, Thomas A. Scott, and Scott's two junior officers, George B.

Roberts and Alexander J. Cassatt. Scott would normally have been the first choice, but there was some doubt among the board members whether he was interested in the position or the most competent alternative. It was common in that era for an executive to pursue both corporate and independent activities, and Scott was so involved in an outside project, the ill-fated Texas and Pacific Railroad, that there was some doubt whether he would accept the position even if it were offered to him.

Born in Franklin County, Pennsylvania, Scott did not receive a formal education, but worked a series of clerical jobs beginning in a toll collector's office and finally, after several unsuccessful business ventures, entered PRR employment in 1850 at age 27. Scott's most endearing quality appears to have been his charm; he was a man of handsome appearance and even temperament who was affable, friendly and unassuming, features not often found in railroad executives then or now. He would have been a successful diplomat, and that is how the PRR used his talents before state legislatures. During the Civil War, Scott was commissioned a colonel and appointed Assistant Secretary of War to supervise railways. He seems to have had traits that neatly complemented his president, performing duties that the gruff, shy Thomson disliked, as well as a talent for organization, and the team of Thomson and Scott successfully managed the PRR through its period of greatest expansion. Scott was the face and voice of the Pennsylvania Railroad for much of the Thomson administration.

George B. Roberts (1833–1897), president of the Pennsylvania Railroad (1880–1897) and warden of the Port of Philadelphia (Photo from the *Centennial History of the Pennsylvania Railroad*, reprinted with permission from the Pennsylvania Historical and Museum Commission and the Railroad Museum of Pennsylvania).

In contrast, George Roberts and Alexander Cassatt were well-educated. Roberts matriculated at Rensselaer Polytechnic Institute when he was 15 and completed its three-year engineering course in two years. Cassatt was educated in Europe before entering Rensselaer and receiving his engineering degree at the age of 20. Both began their PRR careers as rodmen in the survey corps, and both advanced through various engineering and operating positions. In 1880, on the retirement of Scott, Roberts was elected president, and Cassatt, now feeling that he had been passed over twice, resigned and retired to his Lower Merion horse farm. He would later return as president, elected by the board on June 9, 1899, following the death of Roberts. His compensation for 19 years of exile was supervising the planning and design of Manhattan's Penn Station, arguably the most beautiful railroad station ever built in the United States, or perhaps anywhere.[1]

One can imagine the tension in the executive offices of the Pennsylvania Railroad in 1874 after Scott's appointment as president, with the engineers Roberts and Cassatt unimpressed no matter how much charm the Colonel showed them, and Scott feeling a little intimidated by Roberts and Cassatt's shared professional and educational backgrounds, their technical expertise and self-confidence. Scott would have felt much more comfortable in the company of politicians, and when they complained to him of not having a downtown Philadelphia station, he would have been more willing to offer them one, not only to please his politician friends, but also to exercise his authority by overriding the operational objections that Roberts and Cassatt no doubt would have raised. Broad Street Station may have represented the outcome of a test of wills rather than a considered business decision, and the PRR had to live with it for another seven decades.

Broad Street Station also had a profound impact on the region's freight rail system, as the delays that its stub-end design caused for intercity passenger trains happened to occur in close proximity to the PRR's Zoo (or Mantua) Junction, described in 1959 by the Philadelphia City Planning Commission as one of the busiest railroad junctions in the world. By 1900, the Pennsylvania Railroad could be imagined as almost a tangent of main line tracks from New York City to Chicago via Philadelphia, with an extension down from Philadelphia to Washington, D.C., and with all of its New York passenger and freight traffic funneling through Zoo Junction. The PRR developed an extensive system of freight yards just west of Zoo Junction, beginning on the site of what had been its Centennial Fairgrounds satellite yard. These included two 75-acre classification yards, one on either side of 52nd Street, which were crossed by a railroad overpass, plus multiple round houses, crew houses, team tracks, freight transfer terminals and warehouses, repair shops, and later a terminal of its subsidiary Pennsylvania Truck Lines and Mail Van intermodal facility. On nearby Marion Avenue, the PRR's records center occupied a very large factory building, originally home of the Standard Roller Bearing Company. West Philadelphia was a major center of employment on the Pennsylvania Railroad, with many of its predominantly Irish workers—the Aylmers, Maguires and Fayes—living in the Parkside neighborhood within walking distance of the yards and their parish church, Saint Gregory's, on 52nd Street with its parochial school on Lancaster Avenue. In order to provide them with recreation, the PRR replaced its Fairgrounds station with a workers' ball field, to become the home of the Philadelphia Stars of the Negro National Baseball League from 1933 until 1948.

It was necessary for the PRR's New York-Chicago, Pittsburgh-Washington and Schuylkill Valley Line passenger trains to pass through this yard complex as well, so the railroad created a second, higher level of overhead passing tracks with the adjacent 52nd Street passenger station to separate the grade of the passenger trains above the slower freight trains, the passenger line running on the overpass above the freight line, itself on an overpass above 52nd Street. This tiered rail yard was still not enough to relieve traffic congestion, so in 1892, the PRR constructed a 45-mile-long bypass around Philadelphia, known as the Trenton Cutoff, leaving the main line at Trenton and passing north of Philadelphia through Fort Washington like the hypotenuse of a triangle to join the Philadelphia-Pittsburgh corridor at Glen Loch, Pennsylvania, over which all freight traffic between New York and the West was then diverted. One can only imagine the volume of activity that the PRR, and American railroads generally, routinely handled in 1900 and the importance of trains at that time to the average American traveler and shipper.

References

1. George H. Burgess and Miles C. Kennedy, *Centennial History of the Pennsylvania Railroad* (Philadelphia: The Pennsylvania Railroad, 1949), includes a description of Broad Street Station, a discussion of operational problems and attempted remediation, and biographic information on PRR presidents Thomson, Scott, Roberts and Cassatt.
2. Nicholas B. Wainwright, *History of the Philadelphia Electric Company, 1881-1961* (Philadelphia: The Philadelphia Electric Company, 1961), discusses railroad electrification on the Paoli and Chestnut Hill Lines.
3. Philadelphia City Planning Commission, *Philadelphia Railroads* (Philadelphia: PCPC, Comprehensive Planning Division, 1959), includes descriptions of railroad facilities and the Zoo Junction in 1959.
4. Philadelphia City Planning Commission, *The Plan for Center City* (Philadelphia: PCPC, 1988), gives an analysis of impacts on the City of Philadelphia of the development of Penn Center in the 1950s, and the impact of the Liberty Place project on Center City planning.
5. George Wharton Pepper, *Philadelphia Lawyer: An Autobiography* (Philadelphia: J.B. Lippincott, 1944), includes an account of life in the Rittenhouse Square neighborhood in the 1870s.
6. Allen P. Underkofler, ed., *The Philadelphia Improvements, Part I: The Idea and Projects East of the Schuylkill River,* and *Part II: 30th Street Station* (Bryn Mawr, PA: Pennsylvania Railroad Technical and Historical Society, 1979), gives a description of Broad Street

Station's operational problems and attempted solutions, and of planning for Suburban and 30th Street Stations and the Benjamin Franklin Parkway.

7. James J.D. Lynch Jr., *The Chestnut Hill and Fort Washington Branches* (Bryn Mawr, PA: Pennsylvania Railroad Technical and Historical Society, 1997 reprint), includes the story of the development of the Chestnut Hill Branch and Germantown Junction.

8. Francis Burke Brandt and Henry Volmar Gummere, *Byways and Boulevards In and About Historic Philadelphia: The Official Historic Auto-Guide, Sesqui-Centennial Souvenir Edition* (Philadelphia: Corn Exchange National Bank, 1925), gives a good description of the proposed 30th Street Station.

9. Thom Nickels, *Philadelphia Architecture* (Mount Pleasant, SC: Arcadia Publishing, 2005), includes descriptions of architecture along the parkway.

10. Federal Writers' Project, *WPA Guide to Philadelphia,* compiled by the Works Progress Administration for the Commonwealth of Pennsylvania, 1937 (Philadelphia: University of Pennsylvania Press, 1988), gives descriptions of North Philadelphia Station, North Broad Street Station and the Benjamin Franklin Parkway.

11. Russell F. Weigley, ed., *Philadelphia: A 300-Year History* (New York: W.W. Norton, 1982), discusses the Benjamin Franklin Parkway and the planning and development of Penn Center.

12. James L. Holton, *The Reading Railroad: History of a Coal Age Empire, Vol. 2: The 20th Century* (Laury's Station, PA: Garrigues House, 1992), includes a discussion of the Reading's North Philadelphia Station.

13. Anthony R. Sloan and John W. Blatteau, *Reestablishing the Link: A Study of the Commuter Rail Station* (Philadelphia: SEPTA, 1970), gives a good account of the Reading's Wayne Junction Station.

14. Philadelphia City Planning Commission, *Pattison Avenue East Redevelopment Area Plan* (Philadelphia: PCPC, April 20, 1955), includes a useful description of "The Neck."

15. Isador Lichstein, ed., *The Bulletin Almanac* (Philadelphia: *The Evening and Sunday Bulletin,* 1970, 1971, 1972), provides statistical sources from Dun and Bradstreet on numbers of manufacturing firms within the City of Philadelphia.

16. U.S. Department of Labor, Bureau of Labor Statistics, Philadelphia Manufacturing Employment in 1990 and 2011.

17. The John Evans Sons, Inc. website provides a history of the Evans company from 1850 to the present.

CHAPTER 6

30th Street Station

The Pennsylvania Railroad's selection of its 30th Street yards as the location for its new station constituted one of the most significant and complicated land-use decisions ever made in Philadelphia. It was symbolic of the PRR's prowess and confidence at that time in being able to assemble and command the financial, technical and political capital necessary for its implementation. The company's confidence was reinforced by its recent successful participation with three other railroads in the planning and construction of Chicago's Union Station, a project on a scale of cost and complexity similar to what the PRR expected to experience in Philadelphia.

The core problem to be solved in Philadelphia was to find a way to decouple the PRR's intercity through traffic from its local commuter trains originating and terminating here, in a manner that was politically acceptable to its home city and made economic and operational sense to the railroad. It will be recalled that once before in 1864, the PRR had found its own operational solution to downtown delays with its 30th and Market Street Station and its magnificent 1876 Centennial Station at 32nd and Market Streets, only to be drawn back across the Schuylkill in 1881 because of the political and popular uproar over lost downtown service, and then to suffer for the next several decades the consequences of its decision to build Broad Street Station. This was an experience that the PRR had no intention of repeating.

There were other problems needing to be addressed as well. The PRR had grown into a mammoth corporate enterprise, with all the office functions that such a business would entail. By 1920, it had become one of Philadelphia's largest tenants of office space, spread out over many inconvenient locations. Another problem specific to the proposed 30th Street site was the condition and appearance of the public infrastructure that travelers would see and use in the station's vicinity. The general vicinity of the proposed station was at that time home to rather rough, unattractive industrial areas, such as lumber, coal- and stockyards—what today's zoning code would label least restricted uses, and the infrastructure serving the area had a corresponding rundown appearance. Market Street's bridge over the Schuylkill was old and worn, and the Philadelphia Rapid Transit's Market Street Elevated Line alongside was on an unsightly trestle, while PRR plans called for the elevated line to be depressed into a tunnel, as much for aesthetic as operational reasons. The city would need to be coerced or gently persuaded, whichever was necessary, to construct two new crossings of the Schuylkill to the station's front door. In this new station project, the PRR would need partners, and they might need some convincing.

The Pennsylvania Railroad entered into negotiations with the City of Philadelphia to bring them into the project and share responsibilities, and the result was the Terminal Agreement of July 1925. This ordinance dealt with removal of the PRR's Filbert Street Line to Broad Street Station, the demolition of two stations, the construction of bridge and subway facilities, and the new pattern of streets, yards, and track and passenger terminals that would result from this project. Under this agreement, both the city and the PRR undertook to make a series of major changes in the section bounded roughly by Broad Street, Girard Avenue, 47th Street, Woodland Avenue and South Street. These major improvements included all the changes in streets, highways, utilities, bridges, transit facilities, track and yards necessary for the operation of the improvements that the PRR proposed. For example, the city agreed to purchase a portion of the site of the Broad Street Station for "street or parkway purposes only," to widen 15th and 16th Streets, to improve the bridges over Market Street and Chestnut Street, to place Pennsylvania Boulevard (later renamed John F. Kennedy Boulevard) on the street system, to construct a bridge connecting Pennsylvania Boulevard with 30th Street Station, to construct transit improvements including a subway under the route of the Market Street Elevated (in order to provide transit access to the new 30th Street Station) and to demolish the Market Street Elevated Line. The PRR agreed to pay a portion of the cost of the rebuilding of the Market Street and Chestnut Street bridges made necessary by the construction of the new station. For the City of Philadelphia, this was both a huge opportunity and an enormous expense.[1 3 4 5]

Technological innovations presented the PRR with opportunities for improvements unimaginable in 1876, most notably electrification of all passenger service in Philadelphia, but the city could counter that the old station could just as easily be electrified, as it already had been for the 20-mile Paoli and the 12-mile Chestnut Hill Lines, without building a new station. But the PRR would hold the trump card in its negotiations with the city, as the public was now clamoring for removal of Broad Street Station's approaches so that the Ben Franklin Parkway could be completed to Centre Square. There was a new idea as well: that the parkway be linked from City Hall westward to the Schuylkill by another proposed boulevard to connect with an extended East River Drive. Looking back on this 1925 Agreement, the Philadelphia City Planning Commission described it in 1959 as an excellent example of the complexity of the city-railroad relationship, adding that the land made available by it for both public and private use was a "simply incalculable" contribution to the downtown scene.

The Pennsylvania Railroad, comfortable by now with electrification because of its successful experiences in New York and Philadelphia, began planning for its new all-electric station in 1923, after a fire destroyed Broad Street Station's train shed. Under the 1913-to-1925 presidency of Sam Rea (1855–1929), the PRR defined the project, which it named the Philadelphia Improvements, as broadly having four components. These included an intercity, entirely through-track West Philadelphia station with PRR offices and an upper platform for suburban trains; a downtown, below-grade, stub-end-track suburban station with PRR and commercial offices above; another PRR office building in West Philadelphia; and the expanded electrification of lines.

Implementation of the Philadelphia Improvements fell to Rea's successor, General William W. Atterbury (1866–1935), president of the PRR from 1925 to 1935. Atterbury, son of an attorney who was also a Presbyterian home missionary, had graduated from Yale University's Sheffield Scientific School in 1886, and then signed on at the PRR to undertake their four-year apprenticeship program. By 1893, he had become the railroad's Master Mechanic, and in 1911, its Vice President, Operations. When the United States entered World War I, Atterbury had been "drafted" by the War Department as Brigadier General and designated Director-General of Transportation of the American Expeditionary Forces, effectively running the French railroad system in the American zone of operations.

The first and least complicated component of the Philadelphia Improvements that the Atterbury administration addressed was the independent office building. This structure, given the classically Calvinist name of the West Philadelphia Office Building, was to be built in two stages at 32nd and Market Streets. Perhaps getting the idea from the residences in the nearby Powelton and Spruce Hill neighborhoods, the office building was designed as a semidetached structure, or in Philadelphia

General William W. Atterbury (1866–1935), president of the Pennsylvania Railroad (1925–1935) and implementer of the Philadelphia Improvements Program (Photo from the *Centennial History of the Pennsylvania Railroad*, reprinted with permission from the Pennsylvania Historical and Museum Commission and the Railroad Museum of Pennsylvania).

parlance, a "twin." The first half of the twin consisted of 14 stories and 350,000 square feet of usable space in the shape of the letter E facing north, and was completed in 1926. The second half was never constructed, which is the reason why this building presents a blank façade toward Market Street, the footprint of the aborted second stage, now the incongruous site of a tire store. On completion of the first stage in 1926, the PRR relocated many office functions and over 5,000 employees into it, but retained its corporate headquarters at Broad Street Station.

The next phase of the Philadelphia Improvements was construction of the suburban train station and office building. The PRR commissioned the architectural firm of Graham, Anderson, Probst & White, which had designed the PRR's Chicago Union Station, to design its Philadelphia Suburban Station. Construction on this Art-Deco station and office building commenced in July 1927. Extending along the

Philadelphia Improvements Program installments at 30th Street, circa 1950. The station is in the right center, with the West Philadelphia Office Building west of it on Market Street and the power plant on the right to the north of the station. At the time this photo was taken, the Market-Frankford Line had not been relocated into its tunnel under the Schuylkill River. Across Market Street from the station is Philadelphia's main post office, a major Depression-era public works project that has since been converted into offices. The building in the left foreground, now Philadelphia's Marketplace Design Center, showcasing home furnishings, was at the time a Hudson automobile assembly plant. In 1915, this city-owned site, vacant at the time, was proposed for a new municipal convention hall and extension of East River (now Kelly) Drive, complicating the PRR's plans to expand Broad Street Station (Courtesy of The Library Company of Philadelphia).

north side of what at the time was Filbert Street, and from 16th to 17th Streets, Suburban Station consists of eight tracks at a level 35 feet below street grade, above which is the station, itself 15 feet below street grade, over which rises a 22-story, 665,000-square-foot office building. The station is accessed by stairs and elevators from the street grade and the office building, but also by an extensive underground concourse, one of the largest in the United States. Railroad access to the station from west of the Schuylkill is over a four-track bridge designed by Paul Phillipe Cret.

Suburban Station, a stub-end terminal, could not open without a corresponding intermediate station at 30th Street, and a problem arose with construction delays there, necessitating use of a temporary platform so as not to delay Suburban Station's scheduled grand opening in September 1930. To head off the expected complaints from downtown riders that the new station at 30th Street was on the "wrong side" of the Schuylkill, the PRR announced that Philadelphians with tickets on intercity trains could ride free between Suburban and 30th Street Stations upon presenting their tickets to the commuter train's conductor.[4]

Coinciding with the planning and design of Suburban Station, the PRR announced, in March 1926, its intention to electrify its tracks from Philadelphia to Wilmington, and to West Chester via Media. This was wonderful news for Philadelphia Electric Company, which had that same month initiated construction of its mammoth Conowingo Dam hydroelectric power station on the Susquehanna River. But joy in the PECO boardroom turned to angst and dread when the PRR, one of its largest customers, followed with a second announcement in February 1927 that it intended to build its own power station on the Delaware River near Trenton to supply all of the power for its electrification plans. This was only a PRR negotiating ploy, but it worked. In July, the Pennsylvania Railroad agreed to purchase all of its power for the next 20 years from PECO, generated at 60 cycles converted to 25, 13,000 volts, single-phase as before. Up until that time, this was the largest contract that a railroad had ever executed with a utility. The electrification of the Philadelphia-to-Wilmington line was completed in 1928, and in April 1931, the PRR announced that it would now complete electrification on the full Northeast Corridor from New York to Washington, placing on order 90 electric passenger locomotives and 62 freight locomotives. Through electric passenger train service, inaugurated between New York and Washington on February 10, 1935, the travel time of the *Congressional Limited* was cut from four and a quarter hours to three and three-quarters hours, and the Philadelphia-to-New York trip was reduced five minutes to one hour and 40 minutes. At this time, the PRR began electrifying its east-west main line between Paoli and Harrisburg, supported with Depression-era loans from the Reconstruction Finance Administration and the Public Works Administration to stimulate employment and improve infrastructure.[6]

The final and certainly most difficult phase was design and construction of Pennsylvania Station at 30th Street, as it was officially named. First, the site had to

Suburban Station (Author's photo).

be cleared. The location proposed for the new station was occupied by the West Philadelphia Market House, where the PRR received its inbound perishable traffic. The railroad began planning a state-of-the-art perishable terminal, to be located on Oregon Avenue, consisting of a multistory cold storage warehouse and two rail-served produce sheds with tracks along their sides, each having a headhouse whose second floor was occupied by an auction room illuminated with skylights. Construction of this Perishable Products Terminal began in 1927. The multistory warehouse and one of the two sheds, since converted to a cold storage warehouse, still survive at the time of this writing, although the multistory building is in poor condition. The author managed the demolition of a portion of the other building, Shed A's headhouse, in 1993. This complex remained in active use until the early 1970s.

The focus of the 30th Street Station plan was that the main concourse would extend east to west at street grade, with a clear-span coffered ceiling suspended 95 feet above the floor from roof trusses. Its east and west elevations were graced with colonnaded porticoes with Corinthian columns. The upper-level suburban station platform was located on its north elevation for trains to and from Suburban Station, and early plans called for a Market Street Subway-elevated line to have a corresponding station on the south elevation that would be symmetrical with the suburban train station. The elevated station idea was dropped as it was concluded that it would detract from 30th Street Station's esthetic appearance. Instead, the Pennsylvania Railroad proposed that the city and Philadelphia Rapid Transit relocate the elevated line into a tunnel that would pass under both the Schuylkill River and a new, desired Market Street bridge. This choice left the PRR open to the mercy of the fortunes of its partners, the city and the PRT. With the stock market crash, the Depression and World War II, it would be 25 more years before the station's southern elevation could appear as designed.

With the PRR under operational deadlines to have its Suburban Station and offices completed and open for business, the railroad decided to construct 30th Street Station sequentially with the suburban platform first. This was completed on schedule, and the intercity portion of the station was partially finished by the end of 1933. But it would take another two decades for installation of all 10 intercity tracks below the grade of the main waiting room. All phases of the project, including the subway tunnel, the new Market Street bridge and removal of the old PRT bridge, were finally completed in 1956.

The station design incorporated a central control room or interlocking tower on the fourth floor, managing all trains operating through the station originally by means of an electropneumatic system. A fifth floor was used for records storage. Its

West elevation of Pennsylvania Station at 30th Street (Photo by Leigh W. Duffy).

roof was designed to take the weight of aircraft, and was considered to be one of several potential sites for a city heliport projected for 1982. North of the station, the complex included construction of a steam plant, also designed by Graham, Anderson, Probst & White, to provide central heating for both 30th Street and Suburban Stations. This plant was interconnected with PECO's steam heating system, to which the PRR sold steam, beginning in 1934. This steam plant was demolished in 2009.

The station's exterior is of Alabama limestone with base and trim of granite, and its interior is lined with Italian travertine marble above a Tennessee marble floor. Ten octagonal chandeliers, approximately 18 feet long and five feet in diameter, hang from the red-and-gold ceiling. In a waiting room annex to the north of the main waiting area is Karl Bitter's mammoth bas-relief plaque, "Spirit of Transportation," a panoramic relic transferred from Broad Street Station where it had been installed during the 1894 expansion. This annex served as the interim main waiting room during the protracted completion of the station, and today it is occasionally used for dinner parties and ceremonies.

Construction of the 30th Street Station complex was a complicated undertaking because of complex geotechnical conditions encountered in tunneling and bridging the Schuylkill and compensating for vibration in office buildings over railroad terminals. In addition, while construction was under way, trains continued to operate through the 95-acre site, with passengers continuing to board and depart at the old 32nd Street railroad station and walk to and from the new Suburban platform, and

East elevation of 30th Street Station, with the Cira Center in the background (Photo by Leigh W. Duffy).

the PRR would not allow construction activity to penalize service. Construction occurred just after the peak in American passenger rail traffic, although this was not recognized at the time. After a burst of war-related traffic in the 1940s, 30th Street Station shared the fate of the Pennsylvania Railroad and Penn Central, with declining use and revenue leading to deferred maintenance and increasingly haphazard service until the creation of Amtrak. It was most fortuitous for the City of Philadelphia that the Philadelphia Improvements occurred not a moment too soon, as unforeseen conditions would quickly overwhelm the PRR and preclude it from investing in any such magnificent passenger projects ever again.[5]

The railyards around 30th Street Station came back to popular attention when a citizens' panel was convened in 1964 to discuss preparations for a 1976 Bicentennial exhibition, tentatively called the Expo. As had happened in planning the 1926 Sesquicentennial, there was an immediate difference of opinion as to whether this celebration should take the form of an international exhibition located on a large fairground, or a more modest local event. In a planning session for the 1926 event held by Mayor-elect W. Freeland Kendrick in December 1923, Senator George Wharton Pepper; Samuel Vauclain, president of the Baldwin Locomotive Works; and Edward T. Stotesbury, chairman of the Reading Railroad, had argued for a purely local celebration on an "Old Home Week" theme, celebrated at the Fairmount Park's Centennial fairgrounds and at Philadelphia's historic attractions. This concept had won the vote of 403 of the civic leaders present, with only 46 in favor of an international world's fair, but powerful political interests, financially backed by building contractors who would benefit from the costlier alternative, caused the city to opt for an exhibition.[6] This was then sited on a thousand acres of swamp adjacent to the Navy Yard at the foot of Broad Street, guaranteeing lucrative fill contracts for political boss and construction contractor William Vare and his associates. Costing the City of Philadelphia $9.7 million, the "Sesqui" opened on May 31, 1926, but work on some buildings and exhibits was not completed until July 15th. It rained that summer more than half the time, and attendees returned home with negative impressions of Philadelphia. The signature event of the Sesquicentennial, the Dempsey-Tunney boxing match, dismayed the Quakers. Bad memories of that unhappy event still lingered in 1964. Despite that history, a faction of the Bicentennial planning panel known as the Young Philadelphians pressed for an international fairground to be built over the 30th Street Station yards at an estimated cost of $1.2 billion, which it was hoped would be the federal government's contribution to the event.

The enthusiasm of the Young Philadelphians for the Bicentennial was not matched in the rowhouse neighborhoods of Philadelphia, where people viewed the event with the suspicions that characterized the 1960s. Who would benefit and who would pay? What, strangers coming into my neighborhood? In 1971, Philadelphians elected Frank Rizzo mayor, and his preference, like those of his supporters, was a downsized event where the benefits would be immediate and local. Under the direction of his capable City Representative, Eve Asner, sister of the actor Ed Asner, the city embarked on a series of highly successful, well-attended, large-scale entertainment events along the Ben Franklin Parkway that left attendees with an impression of Philadelphia as a lively, vibrant place. Modest venues such as the Mummers Museum, the African American History Museum, the Living History Museum and Remo Saracini's Design for Fun were created more for local consumption. The mistakes of 1926 would not be repeated, and development over the 30th Street Station yards would have to await another opportunity. Philadelphia's Bicentennial celebration's reputation was severely damaged by the outbreak of Legionnaires' disease at Philadelphia's premier tourist hotel, and by Mayor Rizzo's bombastic claim that radical hordes were about to occupy the city during the July Fourth weekend, but entertainment mega-events still continued, better attended than ever, as a testament to Eve Asner's foresight.

One disappointment that befell the Rizzo Administration was its inability to have the proposed Airport High-Speed Rail Line completed and open in time for the Bicentennial. Ms. Asner and her staff had been counting on this line to bring Bicentennial air travelers quickly and efficiently into the downtown area, but the city's plans ran afoul of Amtrak's Northeast Corridor Improvements Program. Simply put, Philadelphia International Airport and 30th Street Station are on opposite sides of Amtrak's Northeast Corridor. Beginning in the late 1960s, at a time when the Penn Central still owned the corridor, the design developed under the direction of Nicholas Bubernak of the city's engineering corps, the Department of Public Property, envisioned the use of an existing commuter rail line running south and west from 30th Street Station's suburban platform. It would merge onto the Amtrak Northeast Corridor near the University of Pennsylvania's Franklin Field, and then gradually, by a system of electronically controlled switches or interlocks, shift the airport train eastward across all of the station's intercity approach tracks at grade to finally reach another track, the old Chester Branch of the Reading Railroad that once had been the Philadelphia, Wilmington and Baltimore Railroad's access from the south into Grays Ferry (see Chapters 2 and 3). Meanwhile, Amtrak, having come to control the Penn Central Corridor, was working to secure commitments of funding to upgrade its track and thus the speeds of its trains on the Northeast Corridor. Amtrak was aggressively planning removal of every speed impediment along its entire right-of-way, and this primarily meant removal of interlocking switches that delayed Amtrak's trains. In the middle of Amtrak's major switch removal campaign, the City of Philadelphia proposed adding four switches and possibly as many as five minutes onto its schedule, and Amtrak's answer to Mayor Rizzo's transportation coordinator Brian Feldman was a resounding no.

This was not the response Frank Rizzo expected to hear from his new friends in Washington. Elected mayor as a Democrat, a short while after his inauguration,

Mayor Rizzo must have undergone a life-changing experience, reminiscent of the
Apostle Paul on the road to Damascus, when he joined Richard M. Nixon's
Committee to Re-Elect the President ("CREEP"). Unlike Paul, he expected an
earthly reward for his conversion, but now Amtrak was telling his engineers that if
they wanted their Airport Line project to proceed, they must design a "fly-over"
bridge overpassing the Northeast Corridor from one side to the other, adding a
decade and many millions of dollars of expense to the Airport Line's completion.
Perhaps Mayor Rizzo's bitter and full-throated rage at what he regarded as his
CREEP friends' duplicity may have been a factor in Transportation Secretary
William Coleman's decision to fund the Center City Commuter Connection
Tunnel.

The Philadelphia City Planning Commission's 1988 *Plan for Center City*
expanded the traditional definition of downtown Philadelphia as extending from
"Vine to South, river to river" by, among other things, crossing the Schuylkill and
addressing the 30th Street Station railyards in its Market Street West District Plan,
thus focusing developer attention on an area that had so often been "mostly viewed
in passing but not really seen." The plan noted that this area's excellent access to all
forms of passenger transportation made it a new frontier for Center City growth
that had the promise of drawing office development across the Schuylkill River into
West Philadelphia. The *Plan for Center City*, more a series of policy recommendations
than the Planning Commission's 1963 edition, which stressed "big projects,"
proposed maximizing the station yards' development potential by rehabilitating the
station itself, improving transportation access, and encouraging new buildings over
the railyard in order to take advantage of dramatic waterfront views and excellent
access to highways, trains and the airport. The many steps proposed by the Planning
Commission to encourage this development are listed in their plan and are not
repeated here.[7]

The 30th Street Station has since undergone renovation and expansion of its
retail features to such an extent that it now has become a destination itself, with
couples taking the train to the station for lunch or dinner, leaving the car at home.
The station yards' first high-rise commercial office building, Cira Center, attests to
the value of 30th Street's transportation and aesthetic attributes. Designed by César
Pilli and completed in 2005, Cira Center includes a bridge linking it to the station.
Its striking form is illuminated with color-changing LED lights over most of its
façade. Its modernist design, so unlike downtown Philadelphia to its east, is
accentuated by its location apart from and in contrast to the mass of Center City's
more conventional high rises. The conversion to offices of Philadelphia's nearby
General Post Office, similar to the station in design and scale, has added more
travelers for the station and shoppers for its retail markets.

Another of the elements of the Philadelphia Improvements, Suburban Station
has continued to show new life and encourage further development nearby. The

wave of 1980s Center City office construction had resulted in many more pedestrians and shoppers visiting the concourse under Suburban Station, and this attracted new retail tenants who improved the attractiveness of the space. The excellent transit access of the concourse attracted more recent office construction, notably the Comcast Center—at 58 stories, Philadelphia's tallest building and, at this writing, the tallest skyscraper in the United States to be awarded the Leadership in Energy and Environmental Design (LEED) designation. It was also given the Urban Land Institute's Award for Excellence as a transit gateway for its connection to Suburban Station. The Comcast Center, designed by Robert A.M. Stern, officially opened in June 2008.

The electrification program pioneered by the Long Island Rail Road, a PRR subsidiary, was extended from New Haven to Boston in the 1990s for passenger service, but the fate of its electrified freight service was far different. The rail reorganization of the 1970s assigned the former PRR/Penn Central Northeast and Keystone (Philadelphia-Harrisburg) Corridors to Amtrak. This effectively discouraged freight volume with user fees that Conrail considered excessive enough to divert as much traffic as possible to parallel routes of the former Reading Railroad, notably Franklin Gowen's Philadelphia-to-Newark route and the Reading main line to Harrisburg.[8] Conrail considered electrifying these routes, but with the cost not justifying the benefit, it opted to scrap the electric freight engine fleet in 1981, and to remove catenary from the electrified routes such as the Trenton Cutoff that

L. Stanley Crane (1915–2003), regarded as the Consolidated Rail Corporation's most successful chairman and chief executive officer (Courtesy of Conrail).

remained in its possession. Thus ended the largest American experiment with electrified freight train service, not likely ever to be repeated because of the cost of its infrastructure. L. Stanley Crane, Conrail's head at the time of this decision, is considered by many in the rail industry to be Conrail's greatest president. Crane had come to Conrail from the presidency of the Southern Railway, which had merged with the Norfolk and Western to create the Norfolk Southern. The walls of the former Southern Railway's boardroom in Atlanta are decorated with oil portraits of the Southern's presidents as far back as the 1850s, with each president in the foreground and his signature accomplishment, such as a bridge or pier, in the background. Alone among these portraits, Stanley Crane's features the president at night with an illuminated freight yard in the background, a reference to his accomplishments in electrical engineering.

In 1987, the Philadelphia Industrial Development Corporation purchased Conrail's former PRR 52nd Street Rail Yard, adding the site to its land inventory. In 1991, after the removal of the rail infrastructure and electric signal wires left behind by Conrail, PIDC held a groundbreaking ceremony for a client and Stan Crane was invited. Crane was asked about his opinion on the demise of Conrail's electric freight operations, and he was not reticent in voicing his pleasure at seeing them ended, remarking that he had made up his mind to get rid of them during his stint in PRR's electrical engineering department in the early 1960s. Given Mr. Crane's background in electrical engineering at both the Pennsylvania Railroad and the Southern, the fact that he chose to scrap Conrail's electric freight service is telling.

References

1. George H. Burgess and Miles C. Kennedy, *Centennial History of the Pennsylvania Railroad, 1846–1946* (Philadelphia: The Pennsylvania Railroad Company, 1949), discusses planning for the Philadelphia Improvements, and gives biographical information on PRR presidents Rea and Atterbury.
2. Francis Burke Brandt and Henry Volkmar Gummere, *Byways and Boulevards in and about Historic Philadelphia*, Sesqui-Centennial Souvenir Edition (Philadelphia: Corn Exchange National Bank, 1925), discusses the PRR's announcement of intent to build 30th Street Station and the city's plan for the Benjamin Franklin Parkway.
3. Philadelphia City Planning Commission, *Philadelphia Railroads* (Philadelphia: PCPC, Comprehensive Planning Division, August 1959), includes a discussion of the Terminal Agreement of 1925.
4. Allen P. Underkofler, *The Philadelphia Improvements, Part I: The Idea and Projects East of the Schuylkill River* (Bryn Mawr, PA: PRR Technical and Historical Society, May 1979), deals with the planning and execution of Suburban Station and the construction of the West Philadelphia Office Building.
5. Allen P. Underkofler, *The Philadelphia Improvements, Part II: 30th Street Station* (Bryn Mawr, PA: PRR Technical and Historical Society, September 1980), covers the planning and construction of 30th Street Station and the demolition of Broad Street Station.

6. Nicholas B. Wainwright, *History of the Philadelphia Electric Company, 1881–1961* (Philadelphia: The Philadelphia Electric Company, 1961), discusses railroad electrification, power plant construction and planning for the Sesquicentennial celebration.
7. Philadelphia City Planning Commission, *The Plan for Center City* (Philadelphia: PCPC, January 1988) considers the impact of Suburban Station and 30th Street Station on the past and future development of Center City and West Philadelphia.
8. Dale W. Woodland, *The Reading in the Conrail Era, Book I* (Telford, PA: Silver Brook Junction Publishing Company, 1998), gives the best account of the relationship of the two railroads.

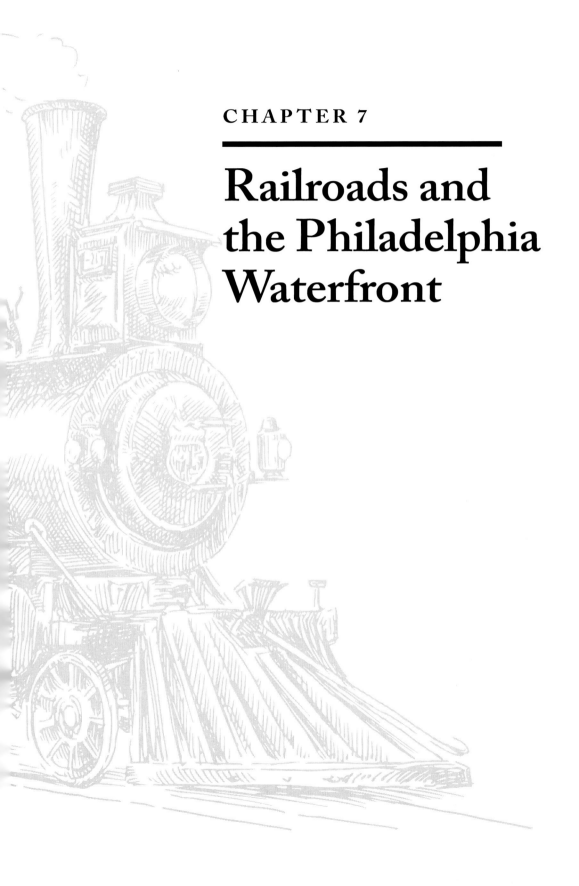

CHAPTER 7

Railroads and the Philadelphia Waterfront

y the 1830s, when railroads began to plan the extension of their lines to the city's waterfront, the Port of Philadelphia was already one and a half centuries old, a mile long, thriving and chaotic, with two-masted coastal shallops laden with hickory, oak, pine and gum vying for berths with clippers in the Liverpool and San Francisco trades, and shipbuilders, warehouses, ferries, taverns, commercial houses, fishermen and even residents jostling for space on the Delaware riverfront. Judging from the names of some of its docks, including Crooked Billet and Broken Wharf, it may have been rather ramshackle, too.

William Penn's original idea was to provide his "greene countrie towne" with a tree-lined river boulevard, but Penn spent little time on his "Holy Experiment," and the pressing interests of commerce soon overrode his wishes. The earliest river road was lined on its west side with lots intended for development of buildings, while its east or riverbank side was decreed to be an open common. By 1690, businesses had expanded across and onto the riverbank side of the street, and the colony's proprietors issued patents allowing this occupancy to continue, but with restrictions on the height of development. The occupants objected to the restrictions and petitioned for their change, which resulted in the Commissioners of the Proprietary formulating what was known as the "Regulation of the Bank." This included the provision that "all owners shall regularly leave 30 feet of ground in the clear, for a cartway and along the said whole bank, and in convenient time shall make the same to be a common and public cartway for all persons, by day and by night, forever hereafter." Thus Water Street was created.

Records indicate that the early maintenance and repair of the city's piers involved public investment, such as a 1704 appropriation by City Council to fund repair of the Arch Street and High (Market) Street wharves. But the city preferred to leave the port in private hands, turning over responsibility to its owners and operators, who formed the Board of Port Wardens at the London Coffee House, located in 1766 at the corner of Front and Market Streets, a board that lasted until 1907. The board had no legal powers and was supported entirely with funds collected from wharf owners and from vessels arriving and departing, until March 1870, when it became a publicly funded city department. In addition to minding the wharves, the wardens operated the quarantine and licensed the river pilots well into the 19th century. Among the early piers was one built for the board in 1773 by Edward Pew on Battery Island in the district of Southwark (below South Street), a structure 35 feet wide and 60 long, dimensions calculated to be able to serve any vessel calling the port at that time. The Board of Port Wardens paid Pew 300 pounds and 60 gallons of rum for his work.

Notable piers and shipping lines in the early 1800s included the Walnut Street Pier, where fully rigged ships of the Cope packet, such as the *Tonawanda, Tuscarora, Wyoming* and *Saranak,* landed their Liverpool passengers and cargo; the Lombard Street wharf, where the firm of Penrose & Burton loaded and discharged its ships,

Dock Street wholesale food market. Dock Street was built over Dock Creek, where William Penn had landed. Dock Street was Philadelphia's principal wholesale food distribution market until 1959, when it was relocated to the Food Distribution Center in South Philadelphia so that the rundown Dock Street neighborhood known as Society Hill could be redeveloped. The Society Hill Towers, now occupying much of the old market area, were designed by I.M. Pei (Courtesy of Philadelphia Industrial Development Corporation).

the *Lancaster* and *Westmoreland*; and the foot of Race Street, where Taylor M. Uhler operated a freight barge service to and from the Delaware and Lehigh Canal. Uhlerstown in Bucks County, along this canal, is named for him. The Cope Brothers' office was located at 1 Walnut Street. The Queen Street Wharf was home to the Southern Mail Line, and the wharves above Market Street were mostly occupied by one of Philadelphia's most famous port wardens, Steven Girard, whose ships, the *Helvetius, Rousseau, Voltaire* and *Montesquieu,* engaged in the French and West Indies trades. With Water Street only 30 feet wide, the Board of Port Wardens decreed that masters of all vessels lying at the piers rig in their jibbooms, which in many instances extended over to the buildings on the western side of the street.

Water Street was still partially occupied by residences, notably the townhouse of Steven Girard at number 43 North, where he entertained many distinguished French refugees, including the statesman Talleyrand and Louis Philippe, the future French king. Also located on Water Street were the mansion of the wealthy miller and landowner William Masters and the townhouse of Pennsylvania Supreme Court Chief Justice William Allen. Allen, one of colonial America's richest men, supported the construction of the State House (now Independence Hall), founded

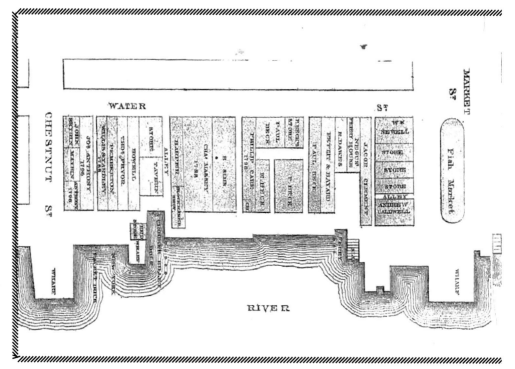

Central Philadelphia waterfront, 1805 (Illustration from *The Port of Philadelphia: Its History, Facilities and Advantages*, Department of Wharves, Docks and Ferries, 1926).

the City of Allentown, helped establish Pennsylvania Hospital, and cofounded the Academy and College of Philadelphia, which later became the University of Pennsylvania. When not residing on Water Street, Chief Justice Allen could be found at his estate, "Mount Airy," in the township of Germantown.[1]

The foot of High (Market) Street was occupied into the 19th century by a wharf that served the nearby Fish Market in the center of High Street and the Jersey Farmers Market. Fishermen, many of whom lived in Camptown along or near the waterfront in Northern Liberties and Penn Township, each had a "gillen skiff" with a "live box" floating astern on arriving at the High Street wharf. These were loaded with shad, eels, perch or "catties" (catfish) for sale by the fishermen at the Fish Market or to the market's hucksters who bought and resold their catch. The Camptowners' favorite fishing spot was Fish House Cove at Petty's Island, across from Camptown, and every family had its eel weir, a low, V-shaped dam of river cobbles thrown up across the mouth of one of the many streams that emptied into the Delaware.

The live box was boat-shaped, about three feet long, closed all around with a hinged door on top and perforated with numerous holes on the sides, keeping the fish alive until wanted. Purchasers would watch as the catfish or eels were skinned

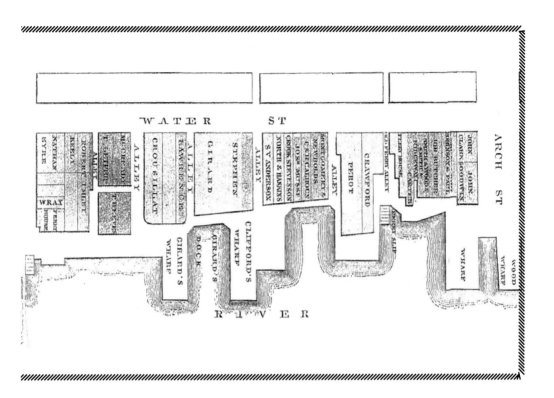

in their presence, thus guaranteeing freshness. Some hucksters trundled their fish home in a wheelbarrow, and early next morning, Sally or Meg would start out with a tray of fish on her head and a basket on her arm, crying "Fresh CATTIES!" as she went from street to street.

Shad in the spring were numerous, selling at retail for 25 cents apiece. Sturgeon were so plentiful that five cents bought two pounds to be smoked for sandwiches. Camptown had its own volunteer fire company, Shad Hose, beginning in 1842. Every block had a "smoker" whose task it was to smoke the shad or herring for the next winter's use. Snappers were plentiful and the first course of many a Philadelphia dinner was snapper soup or stewed snapper. When Charles Dickens visited the United States in 1842, on a mission to plead that publishers respect the copyrights on his books, he was greeted most enthusiastically in Philadelphia with receptions and dinners in his honor, and escorted on a tour around the city. Visiting Camptown, Dickens was so taken with its fishing culture that he exclaimed that it truly was a fish town, and the name stuck.

The women of Fishtown could all swim, fish, row or sail a boat as well as any man. Fishtowners would often sail over to Pea Shore on Fish House Cove and have a shore party. The men would build a campfire from the ready supply of dried

Philadelphia Fish Market, 1837 (Illustration by David J. Kennedy, courtesy of The Historical Society of Pennsylvania).

driftwood along the shore, put on an immense coffee pot and make a "hot pot" of sweetened black coffee with a lump of butter and a shot of rum added to each cup. The women would prepare the ingredients for a snapper soup or "cattiehead stew," potatoes and onions baked in the embers, and fried beefsteak, ham or "flitch" (bacon). When the tide was high, men and women donned old clothes of a light texture and a glorious swim was had by all, young and old. At twilight the fire was doused, camp was struck and they sailed for home, refreshed for the next day's work.

The spring of the year was always a busy time in Fishtown, for during the winter the seines and nets had been repaired, and the toms (buoys fastened to each end of a seine or net) painted. Friends and families banded together to fish for shad, as it required brawn to handle a gillin skiff and pay out or haul in the seine loaded with fish. There was literally cold comfort in fishing offshore, standing in water up to the hips in April and May.[2]

Shipbuilding was a common and profitable activity on Philadelphia's waterfront. As early as 1683, James West established a shipyard at the foot of Vine Street, and by 1793, Philadelphia was producing twice as many ships, measured by tonnage, as any other American city. Joshua Humphreys established a large shipyard in Southwark, which was acquired by the federal government in 1800, and designated the Philadelphia Navy Yard at the foot of Federal Street. There was Hammett's

Screw Dock, where sailing craft were lifted out of the river for repairs by means of a screw or augur, as well as Easby's Smear House Dock, where the hulls of vessels were tarred. Many of these small shipyards failed to make the transition from wood and sail to iron and steam, but one firm that prospered spectacularly during this time was the yard of the Camptowner William Cramp (1807–1879), who moved his operations from Petty's Island to Port Richmond in 1830. Cramp had begun his shipbuilding career and established his reputation as having the best among the 14 shipyards on the Delaware by building fast, wooden clipper ships, but during the Civil War, he made the successful transition to iron ship construction.[1]

The first American iron twin-screw ocean-going steamer, the *Bangor*, was built in 1844 along the banks of the Christiana River in Wilmington, Delaware, in the yards of the Harlan & Hollingsworth Company, up until that time a builder of railroad cars. The river was to the rear of the car builder, and its proximity proved fortuitous when the company decided to enter the shipbuilding business. Although designed for the New England coastal trade, the *Bangor* was purchased by the federal government in 1845, renamed the *USS Scourge*, and used in the Mexican War. In the 1840s, the value of an iron ship was not yet apparent, as Delaware white oak was plentiful and cheaper, but after the 1862 Civil War engagement between

William Cramp (Courtesy of Independence Seaport Museum, William Cramp & Sons Ship and Engine Building Company Collection).

the ironclads *CSS Virginia* (better known as the *Merrimac*) and the federal *Monitor*, government contracts for iron ships sustained this nascent industry.[3]

A noteworthy federal commission in Philadelphia during the Civil War was the *USS New Ironsides*, a fully rigged ship with an auxiliary steam engine and an iron hull 12 inches thick at the waterline, built in 1862. The hull of this ship was fabricated by Cramp, and the engines by Merrick & Sons of Philadelphia. Said to have engaged in more combat than any other vessel during the war and to have been hit many times, she suffered no serious damage. The *New Ironsides* was the pride of the U.S. fleet until destroyed by a fire at League Island, Philadelphia, in 1866.[2]

During the Civil War, Confederate privateers and commerce raiders created such disruption that most Union cargo vessels were transferred to foreign flags, and by war's end, American ocean commerce was in foreign hands. The situation in the shipyards worsened as the federal government held fire sale auctions of surplus blockade vessels. Only coastal shipping held any promise, but the South was prostrate and it would take decades for its economy to recover. American shipbuilding did not look like a rewarding investment. The lessons learned by Cramp in building iron ships during the war were not lost, however. William Cramp's son Charles (1828–1913), president of the shipbuilding company from 1879 until 1903, wrote that the yard began building "iron vessels in a comparatively small way" during the Civil War and that the site "became a sort of kindergarten, as most of the workers had to be trained to the work and working appliances had to be designed."[4]

Cramp Shipyard was joined in 1837 by a new neighbor, the Philadelphia and Reading Railroad, which purchased the Joseph Ball estate just to its north. Owing to the exponential growth of anthracite mining, increasing from 365 tons in 1820 to 174,374 tons in 1830, it was abundantly apparent to the P&R's chief engineer, Moncure Robinson, that a tidewater terminal soon would be a necessity if the railroad's coal traffic were ever to reach more distant markets. Because rampant speculation about the P&R's intentions was driving up the value of Delaware river frontage, Robinson conducted a secret survey in 1837 of an access to tidewater from the P&R's proposed line in West Falls, charting a route via Nicetown below Germantown. His instructions were that from Reading on down to tidewater docks in Philadelphia, no portion of the roadway should be more difficult for the locomotive than level, and that no descending grade should be greater than 19 feet per mile, in order that whatever number of loaded coal cars an engine could take down from Schuylkill County, it would be able to bring back that number of empties to the coal region. It is remarkable even today that a track so many miles in length should be constructed without an adverse grade in the direction of its heaviest traffic. Although construction was delayed by unfavorable economic conditions, the P&R opened its Port Richmond Terminal on May 17, 1842. Initially having five piers, within four years it was expanded to 13, making it the largest tidewater rail terminal in Philadelphia.[7]

Port Richmond Terminal, like its developer, was conceived as a coal operation, and as anthracite tonnage continued to grow, the Philadelphia and Reading under President Franklin Gowen decided to gain control over the ocean shipping of coal, and proceeded to acquire iron ships for this purpose. While the P&R attempted to construct some of these ships itself at Port Richmond, the railroad eventually decided to purchase most of them, and Cramp Shipyard was a natural choice for its neighbor. By 1877, Port Richmond Terminal was handling 5,784,657 tons of anthracite, much of it aboard P&R ships built by Cramp.

The shipbuilding industry flickered back to life thanks also to commissions from the Pennsylvania Railroad. A PRR predecessor, the Philadelphia, Wilmington and Baltimore Railroad had first made use of the short Southwark Railroad, constructed in the bed of Washington Avenue, to access the Delaware riverfront. In 1856, before its acquisition of the PW&B, the Pennsylvania Railroad proposed constructing its own line on Washington Avenue, and in 1859, it developed its own shipping terminal at the foot of Queen Street, just north of the Navy Yard. The PRR bridged the Schuylkill and put its own Washington Avenue line into operation in 1861, not a day too soon for the war effort. The terminal was expanded with the addition of coal piers and a grain elevator. Previously, grain had been carted in bags from warehouses on Broad Street and passed into the ship's hold bushel by bushel.

In 1870, the PRR organized the American Steamship Company to operate between Philadelphia and Liverpool, and commissioned William Cramp & Sons to produce four iron ships—the *Pennsylvania, Indiana, Illinois* and *Ohio*—each 355 feet long with a beam of 43 feet, to carry 76 first-class and 854 steerage passengers and 3,000 tons of cargo. All were launched between August 1872 and June 1873. Also in 1873, the PRR extended a line from its Schuylkill bridge directly southward to Girard Point on the east bank of the river and constructed a new terminal there for the Red Star Line, offering to waive their dockage and wharfage charges to make the line's Philadelphia-to-Antwerp service competitive with New York rates. It added a grain elevator there, and began the first of many projects developing Greenwich Point on the Delaware River below Oregon Avenue, where it constructed coal docks. The PRR's track eastward from Girard Point to Greenwich was named the Delaware Extension, skirting along the shore of the back channel above League Island. Once having extended eastward, the track turned northward along the Delaware waterfront to Washington Avenue, completing a belt track encircling South Philadelphia at street grade.

When the Navy relocated its base southward to League Island, the PRR purchased its old Federal Street site for $1 million and expanded there after the Navy's departure in 1876, adding covered general cargo piers, freight sheds and railyards. Also included was an immigrant station. The Pennsylvania Railroad was becoming a major presence in the Port of Philadelphia, and shifting the port's locus southward.[8]

Pennsylvania Railroad Piers 53 and 54, at the foot of Washington Avenue, wharves of the Red Star Line. The PRR built these piers after acquiring the site, the original Philadelphia Navy Yard, from the U.S. Government. Pier 53 was the entry point for thousands of immigrants, ancestors of many of today's Philadelphians—the city's own "Ellis Island" (Courtesy of American Premier Underwriters, Inc.).

Just as Matthias Baldwin made Philadelphia a world-renowned center of locomotive building, William Cramp did the same for shipbuilding, with a varied combination of civilian and military vessels in his order book. By the early 1880s, the Civil War–era Navy's obsolete monitors and wooden sailing vessels had become, in the words of Navy Secretary William Chandler, "a subject of ridicule at home and abroad." After much urging, Congress authorized construction of four steel ships, the cruisers *Atlanta, Boston* and *Chicago*, and the message dispatch vessel *Dolphin*, together known as the "ABCD ships." This was a remarkable decision, given not only that Congress would approve such a large military procurement in peacetime, but also in light of concern that the United States lacked the necessary large-scale steel production. Bids were advertised in 1883, and of the eight bids submitted, only two bidders, William Cramp and John Roach of Chester, took on all four ships. It must have been a pencil-chewing nightmare for the shipyards' estimators, as the final hull design for the *Dolphin* was approved just one hour before the opening of bidding, and the machinery plans for the *Atlanta* and *Boston* were not approved until four days after the contracts had been awarded.

John Roach won what were essentially design-and-build contracts, given the slapdash specifications and constant interference and plan changing by the War

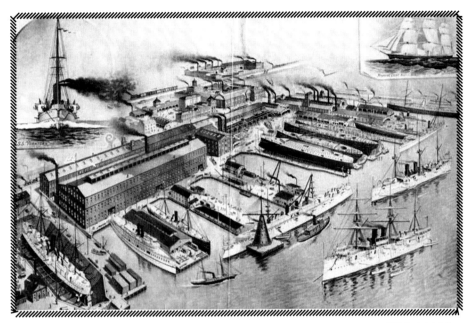

Cramp Shipyard, 1903 (Courtesy of the Print and Picture Collection, Free Library of Philadelphia).

Department, for all four of the ships, but over the strong protests of William Cramp. The awards confirmed yet again the adage of Roach's fellow Irishman Oscar Wilde to be careful about what one wished for. The Republican administration of Chester A. Arthur was succeeded by that of Democrat Grover Cleveland in the election of November 1884. Arthur had been convinced that "there is something radically wrong with the War Department." The Attorney General was persuaded to declare John Roach's contract invalid, and within two years the heartbroken shipbuilder had died. It was now the Cleveland Administration's turn to ruminate on Wilde's truism, as no federal shipyard was capable of completing Roach's contracts. The Navy was forced to seize his shipyard and complete the ships under its own supervision, to Roach's heirs' bittersweet satisfaction.

The Cleveland Administration, determined to put its own stamp on the fledgling steel navy, let out for bids construction of a new cruiser, the *Newark*. This contract was awarded to William Cramp in 1887 and completed in 1891. The lengthy construction was delayed by the Navy's use of obsolete engine designs, which Cramp had to rework. With his updated mill, the *Newark* attained a highly satisfactory 19 knots during her sea trials. He went on to be the successful bidder on the cruisers *Baltimore* and *Philadelphia*, along with many other U.S. Navy warships. Cramp incorporated in 1872, 37 years before Baldwin, as William Cramp & Sons Ship and Engine Building Company began to receive orders from a worldwide buyers' roster.

The company built warships for Japan, the Ottoman Empire and Russia, where William's successor Charles Cramp was decorated by the Czar. It built the U.S. Navy's premier battleship, the *USS Indiana*, in 1893. Cramp built cargo ships for all significant North and South American steamship lines. Among the company's most notable and important creations were the U.S. Navy's only dynamite cruiser, *Vesuvius*, and the new *Maine*, whose keel was laid on the first anniversary of the loss of the original battleship of that name in Havana Harbor. By 1902, under the leadership of Charles Cramp, its shipyard occupied 50 acres in Kensington and, in 1917, achieved its maximum employment of 10,000. In 1925, the company had operations in Chester, New York and San Francisco, in addition to its shipyard and the adjacent I.P. Morris machinery shop in Port Richmond.

Not everything went as planned. On March 25, 1895, Cramp Shipyard was the site of one of the more embarrassing moments in Philadelphia history—some might say even worse than that unforgettable, unforgivable Thanksgiving Day when Philadelphians booed Santa Claus on Market Street during the Gimbels parade. Over 30,000 onlookers attended the launching of the big American Line steamer *St. Paul* for the International Navigation Company, the "Red Star Line," only to gasp in amazement as the vessel got stuck on its skids. Not enough tallow had been

Cramp Shipyard with the *Malolo* under construction, 1925. The building in the lower left foreground, formerly the I.P. Morris Engine Shop, the last remaining Cramp structure, was demolished in 2011 (From a Sesquicentennial brochure from the Department of Wharves, Docks and Ferries in the author's collection).

used to grease them properly. The *St. Paul* was finally launched on April 12th in a private ceremony.

Cramp's last major civilian commission was the *Malolo,* a luxury cruise ship for Matson Navigation Company's Hawaii service, completed in 1926. Under various owners and names, this ship remained in service until the mid-1970s. William Cramp's eponymous company was purchased in 1919 by the American Ship and Commerce Corporation, but by 1919 the Czar and the Ottoman Empire were history and the Imperial Japanese Navy was now building its own warships at Kure in southern Honshu, with tragic results.

The market for ocean freighters was being saturated by another Philadelphia shipyard, built by the American International Shipbuilding Corporation on the Delaware River at Hog Island to produce ships for service in World War I. The Pennsylvania Railroad constructed its 60th Street branch line to the shipyard from its Philadelphia-to-Washington line, and the P&R appended to it a connection from its Chester Branch. Hog Island Shipyard was just hitting its stride, employing 34,000 and capable of building 50 ships at one time, when the Armistice was signed in November 1918. While orders for troop-carrier vessels were then canceled, the U.S. Government sought to cushion unemployment and to revive the merchant marine by completing its orders for cargo vessels, 1,180 freighters being launched in 1919 before Hog Island was finally closed. However, the recession of 1921 was not avoided, nor was the merchant marine revived. The shipyard site was later conveyed to the City of Philadelphia and is now a part of Philadelphia International Airport. Hog Island Shipyard will be forever revered by Philadelphians as the birthplace of the "hoagie" (originally "hogie") sandwich that its workers brought for lunch.

With the signing of the international treaty limiting naval forces in 1923, U.S. Navy orders evaporated and, facing the inevitable, Cramp Shipyard closed in 1927. Phoenix-like, it arose again in 1940, producing cruisers and submarines for the Navy, its very last vessel being the cruiser *USS Galveston,* launched in April 1945. For over a decade afterward, the shipyard remained a padlocked vacant property of the Navy Industrial Reserve until being purchased by the Philadelphia Industrial Development Corporation, which demolished it in 1962 to create an industrial park. The single remaining building from the Cramp era, the I.P. Morris machine shop on Richmond Street, was demolished in 2011.[3]

Cramp's association with Czarist Russia was commemorated in a unique ceremony in February 1992 at Saint Andrew's Russian Orthodox Cathedral at 5th Street and Fairmount Avenue. The event was a remembrance of the 88th anniversary of the sinking of the *Variag,* one of Russia's most famous battleships. Launched at Cramp Shipyard in 1899, the *Variag,* named after the Vikings who emigrated to Russia, was confronted off the Korean coast in 1904. A Japanese fleet of six battleships, six cruisers and 12 torpedo craft demanded the Russian ship's surrender, but the *Variag*'s 550-man crew, ever after known as the Saint Andrew's sailors, fought for "59 minutes of hell," losing 109 officers and men but still returning to port. The Russian Navy later burned the *Variag* to prevent its capture. At this ceremony, for the first time since before the 1917 Russian Revolution, officers of the U.S. and Russian navies came together as friends to celebrate the memory of this heroic ship. The cathedral was an especially appropriate venue, as it had been founded by, among others, Russian sailors assigned as crew members to ships that Cramp was constructing for their navy. A model of the *Variag* is in the collection of the Franklin Institute.[5]

Neither William Cramp nor Matthias Baldwin could have achieved their success without having high-grade steel, and their source was Philadelphia's Midvale Steel Company. Cramp, Baldwin and Midvale were the cornerstones of industrial Philadelphia in the second half of the 19th century, linked together by the Philadelphia and Reading Railroad. Midvale Steel Works, the third anchor of Philadelphia's industrial age, was founded in Nicetown in 1867 as the Butcher Steel Works. Its founder was William Butcher, an immigrant from Sheffield, England, the center of the British steel industry. Butcher's intent was to produce high-quality steel for the American railroad industry. Sheffield was the location where Robert Huntsman had first produced crucible steel in 1740. Huntsman, a clockmaker, was motivated to experiment with steel produced in a container because of his frustration with the crude, poor-quality metal springs and pendulum rods that powered his clocks. He believed that steel created in a crucible would produce ingots that were perfectly homogeneous throughout. With his discovery, Huntsman raised iron mongering from alchemy to metallurgy. However, the difficulty of creating crucibles capable of withstanding the extreme heat that was needed for the process made crucible steel far too expensive for structural or machine applications.

This problem was solved by an American, William Kelly, who was awarded a U.S. patent, and also by Henry Bessemer of Sheffield in 1856. Apparently, each of them made an independent discovery of the process that now bears Bessemer's name. It involves the blowing of air through molten cast iron to oxidize its impurities, using multiple crucibles fed by a common air pipe. This process, which went through

Midvale Steel Works, 1903 (Courtesy of the Germantown Historical Society, Philadelphia, PA).

several refinements to overcome chemical deficiencies, resulted in high-quality, lower-priced steel that could be used affordably in such industrial applications as boiler making, critical to the production of steam engines for locomotives and ships. Steel rails lasting six years could now replace iron rails whose lifespan was three months.[11]

William Butcher chose a site for his works on the line of the P&R, extending from the Schuylkill River at East Falls to the Delaware River tidewater at Port Richmond Terminal, so that the mill could have ready access to the iron and coal being mined along the railroad, and rail access to his Bush Hill market. Butcher died not long afterward, and his place was assumed by the gentleman residing at 1819 Vine Street, William Sellers (see Chapter 1). Sellers, like Robert Huntsman, was acutely cognizant of the need for high-quality, homogeneous steel, so that its reliability would be consistent and could be duplicated for reorders using scientific standards for measuring its qualities.

Known after 1880 as Midvale Steel Company, the mill charted a business plan for itself that was different from other American steelmakers, never aspiring to be a volume producer, but always pushing the state of the art. This was of particular importance to Bush Hill machinists and later to the nascent auto industry, and to the War Department, ever desirous of improving the armor plating of its ships and the accuracy, range and lethality of its artillery. Midvale produced Cramp's armor

William Sellers (From the author's collection).

plate using its own metallurgical formula that won it independence from paying the "Krupp royalty." The mill manufactured artillery barrels and shells for Philadelphia's Frankford Arsenal and steel for Baldwin's Eddystone Ammunition Corporation rifle factory. Midvale even produced much of the steel used in the construction of the Brooklyn Bridge.[9]

In 1915, the Midvale works was joined by a new neighbor, the Edward G. Budd Company. The Delaware-born Budd (1870–1946), possessing a precocious aptitude for mechanics, set off for Bush Hill in 1890 to find his future and was hired by William Sellers, who employed him as a draftsman in his machine shop at 16th and Hamilton Streets. At night, Budd studied at the Franklin Institute on South 7th Street, developing a specialty in welding, only recently invented by N.V. Bernados in Russia in 1887, and with a U.S. patent issued to Charles L. Coffin in 1889. About 1900, Budd joined the firm of Hale & Kilburn, a manufacturer of railroad fixtures located at 6th and Arch Streets, four blocks away from the American Philosophical Society and the Franklin Institute. Among its various products, Hale & Kilburn made the reversible seats needed by railroads servicing stub-end facilities like Broad Street Station and Reading Terminal.

At the turn of the century, automobiles were too costly for any but the wealthy to afford, and these early autos owed much of their styling to the use of aluminum in their bodies. Aluminum was easier to shape than steel, but very expensive, and

Edward G. Budd (center) with executives of the Canadian Pacific Railroad in the mid-1930s (Courtesy of the Pennsylvania Historical and Museum Commission and the Railroad Museum of Pennsylvania).

composite bodies of aluminum, steel and wood were not as strong as an all-steel car body would be. Budd experimented with arc welding and was able to produce superior spot welds on steel that Hale & Kilburn could use in manufacturing railroad passenger equipment. Budd also developed a specialty in metal stamping, another relatively new technology that got off to a curious start in the United States in Budd's home state of Delaware. In 1860 or 1861, two Frenchmen emigrated to Wilmington, smuggling out with them blueprints for a sheet metal press that they had operated in France. The two built their press inside a barn in a completely enclosed room, allowing for only three people to occupy the closely guarded space. Their firm, Higgins & Marchand Company, manufactured a washbasin there that was the first product of stamped sheet metal ever made in the United States. One may conjure a teenaged Edward Budd being admitted to this inner sanctum, observing this secret process with intense curiosity, and in a eureka moment resolving to seek his fortune in metalworking and setting out for Bush Hill immediately. Metal stamping would become a key technology of the auto industry, and Budd and his colleagues were among its principal innovators.

Budd's welding and stamping techniques attracted the interest of Detroit automobile builders, and by 1912, Hale & Kilburn had relocated to a larger factory at 17th and Lehigh, near Midvale, producing auto bodies entirely of steel. In that year, Budd and his partners created his eponymous company. Their big break came in 1914 with a substantial order from the Dodge brothers, and in 1915, Budd moved into his new factory along the Reading's Port Richmond Branch and across from Midvale. The Edward G. Budd Company was one of Philadelphia's most successful businesses of the 20th century, developing assembly plants in Detroit and partnerships in Europe with Morris and Citroen. There were many innovations in welding technology in the century's first two decades, with the introduction of carbon arc, inert gas, thermit, flow, resistance and other processes—and Budd and his partners developed many of them.

Budd created the first American stainless-steel passenger train, the streamlined, three-car *Zephyr* for the Burlington Railroad, commissioning Paul Phillipe Cret to design its interior and the Reading's *Crusader*. In 1937, Budd designed and built a huge, double-decked, stainless-steel, air-conditioned bus trailer furnished with sleeping berths, a "desert cruiser" designed to be towed across the Syrian desert, making the 600-mile run between Damascus and Baghdad in 15 hours, cutting the prior schedule by one-third.[1][7] The company worked closely with Midvale, encouraging it to invest in the oversized electric-arc ovens that Budd needed for its forgings. Budd's order book included a full roster of American auto producers, from Buick to Willys. Its Nicetown plants, expanded along the Port Richmond Branch and west of the PRR's Chestnut Hill Branch, accounted for almost 11,000 outbound rail carloads on the Penn Central alone in 1972, with four switch engine crews assigned by Penn Central to the Midvale Yard to switch Midvale and Budd traffic.

Budd was acquired by the German firm Thyssen in 1978, and in 1999, Thyssen merged with Krupp, Midvale Steel's old nemesis. Thyssen-Krupp consolidated its auto plant operations in Detroit and closed Budd's Nicetown facilities in 2002.[14]

Midvale Works was the laboratory where the father of time-and-motion study, Frederick Winslow Taylor (1856–1915), Midvale's chief engineer in the 1880s, controversially sought to maximize labor productivity by reducing, if not eliminating, workers' extraneous tasks and idle time. The object was to achieve the best possible work pace while rewarding workers with a differential pay rate based upon output. Businessmen applauded Taylor's productivity advances but conveniently ignored his differential pay recommendation. Beginning in 1890, Taylor applied his talents as an efficiency expert to other companies, among them Cramp Shipyard and Bethlehem Steel. He was the recipient of the Franklin Institute's highest achievement award, the Elliott Cresson Gold Medal, in 1902. In 1905 and '06, Taylor was president of the American Society of Mechanical Engineers. Over his lifetime, he was granted over 100 patents.[9]

In the 1880s, it must have been galling for Pennsylvania Railroad's management to watch all of the industrial activity on its rival's system, and they determined to find a way to compete for their share of it. This would involve extension of lines to Cramp and to Midvale, but the intense development of Bush Hill made any inroad there by track construction infeasible. A Philadelphia attorney, not an engineer, would be needed to crack open this opportunity. The connection to Midvale was made from the PRR's Chestnut Hill Branch in 1893 via its 0.7-mile-long Midvale Branch between Westmoreland and Queen Lane Stations. Its attempt to connect to Cramp Shipyard was to have a far-reaching impact on the Port of Philadelphia.

One reason why the Pennsylvania Railroad concentrated its development of port facilities in South Philadelphia was the extreme congestion in the old mile-long central city waterfront between Vine and South Streets. Another was the narrow shipping channel off Chestnut and Walnut Streets that was constrained by Smith's and Windmill Islands in the Delaware River.

The Board of Port Wardens was well aware of the waterfront roadway problem, and Steven Girard, one of America's three richest men, made it his personal mission to correct it. He planned a new waterfront street, Delaware Avenue, and bequeathed $500,000 in his 1831 will, the interest on his bequest to be used to improve and maintain this road. Under an ordinance approved by City Council in 1834, Delaware Avenue was laid out 25 feet wide from Vine to Cedar (South) Streets. Trustees of Girard's will bore the expense of creating and developing this avenue according to his plan from 1834 until 1845.

Between 1857 and 1867, the Girard trustees widened Delaware Avenue to 50 feet. Subsequently, a portion of the thoroughfare fronting on the Queen Street wharf between Dock Street and Delaware Avenue was placed on the city plan at 80 feet wide, and in the central waterfront between Christian and Laurel Streets, above

Spring Garden Street, the width was extended to 150 feet in 1897. The increased width was taken from the docks, the city acquiring over 360 feet of additional waterfront property between Vine and South Streets. South of Washington Avenue, Delaware Avenue was placed on the city plan at a width of from 150 to 250 feet down to the Greenwich piers.

The delivery to the PRR of the *Pennsylvania,* a Cramp ship 355 feet long in August 1872, was a wake-up call to the Board of Port Wardens, echoing the next year when the railroad opened its shipping terminal at Girard Point, four miles south of the historic central waterfront district. Up until the PRR's order with Cramp, ships were built not according to demand for cargo space, but according to the length of the piers where they docked. In Philadelphia's central waterfront, the length of the piers was limited by the proximity of the shipping channel, which could not be blocked by a docked ship. The central waterfront's shipping channel was in turn defined by the proximity of Smith's and Windmill Islands, between Market and South Streets. The PRR's new ships foretold that the central waterfront was doomed to obsolescence unless these islands were removed.

City Council members were prevailed upon by the port wardens to enact an ordinance in June 1878, authorizing appointment of a committee to "devise and present a plan to increase and accommodate the commerce of the Port of Philadelphia." Nine years later, this committee submitted its report recommending the removal of Smith's and Windmill Islands, the extension of wharves and the modification of harbor pierhead and bulkhead lines. The Board of Port Wardens called upon Pennsylvania Railroad president George B. Roberts to initiate the project.

At this time, the port wardens and George Roberts were very much engaged, as Roberts had proposed extending northward his Delaware Avenue track, which ran as far as Dock Street, and the wardens had authorized his creation, the River Front Railroad Company, to build a line in the bed of Delaware Avenue as far north as the Pennsylvania Railroad's Kensington Station, at Kensington Avenue and Berks Street, the southern terminus of the Philadelphia and Trenton Railroad that the PRR had acquired in June 1871. This project was begun in 1881, with the last rail laid in the bed of Delaware Avenue on March 23, 1882. Denied by the Philadelphia and Reading the access that it sought to Cramp Shipyard, the PRR's River Front Line nevertheless secured a "backdoor" connection there in 1890 by way of its Norris Street Line and yard. This connection coupled with its Midvale Branch (1893) provided the PRR competitive if circuitous access for hauling steel between Midvale and Cramp, but Baldwin remained beyond reach on the P&R's Willow and Noble Street Line. The P&R, of course, was denied access to the River Front Railroad, so that the piers between Dock Street and Callowhill Street would remain captive to the Pennsylvania Railroad.

Perhaps the nine-year delay between the port improvement committee's 1878 formation and the issuing of its report in 1887 was attributable to strong, vocal opposition to removal of Smith's Island, home of a famous bathing and beer garden resort known as Ridgway Park, established in the 1820s. This was a popular amusement site where bluestocking Philadelphians could unwind after a long week's work in the courts and commercial houses. Perhaps it was also due to the bare-knuckle competition then under way between the Pennsylvania Railroad and the Philadelphia and Reading playing itself out on the waterfront.

Under George Roberts' energetic leadership, funds were secured from the federal and state governments, and the project of removing Smith's and Windmill Islands, begun in 1891, was completed in January 1894, with the dredged material deposited in the back channel separating the League Island Navy Base from South Philadelphia. But Roberts' involvement also raised a possibility for a windfall PRR benefit at the P&R's expense—monopoly of Philadelphia's commercial waterfront. But with the widening of Delaware Avenue and realignment of the harbor lines, perhaps Philadelphia could have a proper belt railroad accessing all potential shipping points on the belt with competitive rail service provided by all railroads having access to Philadelphia. Other cities were developing similar belt railroads, so why not Philadelphia? The Philadelphia Board of Trade and the Commercial Exchange of Philadelphia were very much in favor of the idea, and they proposed that the belt line cover the entire main waterfront of the city.

Roberts saw that this belt line could also be to his advantage. From the PRR perspective, such a line had the potential to provide his railroad with access not only to Cramp, but perhaps even to Bush Hill if the P&R Noble Street tracks could be negotiated into the belt line. From the outset, the Philadelphia and Reading saw a potential Pennsylvania Railroad waterfront monopoly as among the gravest of threats to its franchise. The P&R had much more to lose than the PRR, and the latter had much more to gain. But the July 1886 completion of the Baltimore and Ohio Railroad connection to Philadelphia, including a line running across South Philadelphia, changed the equation and put the PRR on the defensive. If the Board of Port Wardens could authorize a Pennsylvania Railroad belt track extension northward, how could they deny a petition by the P&R and the B&O for a belt line southward? The defining limits of the belt now became critical.

The Philadelphia and Reading and its allies organized the Philadelphia Belt Line Railroad Company, chartered in 1889, with the goal of creating a belt route alternative to the Pennsylvania Railroad, running entirely around Philadelphia. While such an undertaking might not be economically feasible, the threat that it presented might just induce the PRR to open its own belt system to access by the other railroads. At the very least, it presented the P&R with a bargaining chip that could block PRR access to Bush Hill and Cramp, and a waterfront monopoly. The stage was set for a major confrontation.

The Board of Port Wardens was sympathetic to George Roberts' position. It did not want to see a maze of additional tracks constructed in the bed of central Delaware Avenue, adding to delays and congestion that the board was attempting to resolve. Roberts was adamant that the PRR's tracks and customers would not be opened to servicing by other railroads. Yet the idea of belt line access to the developing South Philadelphia waterfront was certainly desirable for the port's future. A compromise was needed, and under the leadership of Board of Port Wardens director Henry Winsor, of the Winsor Line, an agreement was reached.

To avoid duplicate tracks, the PRR, P&R and B&O agreed in 1892 that another belt line track in the central city waterfront would not be built, but that the PRR would switch P&R and B&O freight cars for them, including switching cars on the PRR's Riverfront Railroad in the central waterfront, a significant concession. Roberts did win a concession from the P&R, allowing for the two railroads to jointly own and operate belt tracks north of Vine Street to Port Richmond Terminal, including a connection to Cramp Shipyard on Richmond Street, but the PRR failed to gain access to the Noble and Willow Street Line to Bush Hill. This 1892 agreement provided for the Pennsylvania Railroad to receive one dollar per loaded car and 50 cents per empty car for switching the other railroads' traffic below Vine Street. These charges remained in effect until 1920. As late as 1971, the Interstate Commerce Commission required that the PRR (by then the Penn Central) be compensated only a total of $5.66 per car. The ICC finally allowed the rate to be raised to $23.56 per car in 1972, but by then the Penn Central's accounting department estimated the true switching cost to be over $48 per car, or a shortfall of $25 per car. In 1972, the Penn Central switched over 8,000 railcars on Delaware Avenue for its competitors at a loss amounting to $200,000. For once the PRR had been outfoxed. In 1892, the neutral Belt Line Railroad built a line from Port Richmond north to Bridesburg so that the P&R could compete with the PRR's parallel and nearby Kensington and Tacony Branch.[1][13]

With the removal of Smith's and Windmill Islands, the realignment of the channel and of pierhead and bulkhead lines, and the widening of Delaware Avenue in 1898, the Port of Philadelphia embarked on a golden age that lasted until the advent of containerized shipping in the late 1950s. In June 1907, the Board of Port Wardens was replaced with the city's Department of Wharves, Docks and Ferries, which was given responsibility for construction, with public funds, of modern pier facilities. In other ports, a trend had become apparent of public agencies constructing piers for general or packet cargo, and of railroads building piers for bulk cargos such as coal, ore and grain, and so the department focused its attention on building general cargo terminals.

At that time, the city owned only three narrow municipal piers, at the foot of Race, Arch and Chestnut Streets, wharves that were used for river traffic only and did not contribute to the port's international commerce. The new department's first project, Pier 19 North at the foot of Vine Street, was completed in 1910. It was, at 166 feet, double the width of the city's previous piers, and its 566-foot length could accommodate the largest ships then being built by Cramp. This was followed in 1915 by the two Southwark piers, 38 and 40, at the foot of Catherine Street on the

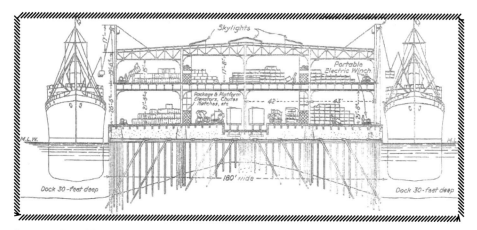

Cross section of Piers 38 and 40 (From a Sesquicentennial brochure from the Department of Wharves, Docks and Ferries in the author's collection).

site of the old Southern Mail Line and PRR wharves, and in 1922 by Piers 3 and 5, where Steven Girard's *Voltaire* once docked. In South Philadelphia, where bulkhead lines created much larger pier sites, the department constructed its Moyamensing piers, numbered 78, 80, 82 and 84, with an adjacent municipal railyard. Pier 84 was constructed in 1925 with a length of 900 feet, a width of 336 feet and a draft alongside of 35 feet. Pier rents were calculated to service the debt owed by the city from borrowing for the piers' construction. All of these piers had rail access via the belt line operated by the Pennsylvania Railroad. The Moyamensing and Southwark piers remain very much in operation today, handling such cargos as paper and cocoa beans, and have paid off their construction debt many times over, while the Girard piers have been converted to condominiums.

With the outbreak of World War I, the federal government's Quartermaster Corps also constructed piers and warehouses in Philadelphia, similar to its Brooklyn and Bayonne terminals, including the Federal Maritime Terminal. This consisted of Pier 98, a hulking, 1,500-foot-long, three-deck structure at the foot of Oregon Avenue, and what would have been its twin, Pier 96. The war ended before Pier 96 was finished, and it was left as an open-deck structure, now used for auto imports. Built in the days before alternating current was accepted, these two piers had their own adjacent direct current electric power station.

The Port of Philadelphia's special advantage after 1907 was that, unlike competing ports, all of its piers used for international shipping had direct rail access switched off the Belt Line and onto tracks that led directly into the enclosed pier or "transit shed," or along the aprons of the piers next to their berths. In the era before truck transport came to dominate general cargo, Philadelphia freight could be transferred on the pier directly from the railcar to the ship without having to "lighter" the cargo, that is, transfer the railcar onto a barge either to transship it to another pier on the waterfront or to unload the railcar from the barge onto the ship. Railroad veteran Tom Collard likes to tell of "the happiest day on the old CNJ" when the Jersey Central Railroad retired its last lighter in New York Harbor. Philadelphia's direct rail-ship transfer capability helped its port overcome the disadvantage of being 80 miles up the Delaware River from the Atlantic Ocean.

While the city's Department of Wharves, Docks and Ferries was fully involved in its general cargo pier construction projects, the Philadelphia and Reading and the Pennsylvania Railroad expanded and improved their own facilities. The P&R's Port Richmond Terminal, described by them as the "largest privately owned tidewater terminal in the world," by 1926 encompassed 10 piers and over 85 miles of track. Pier 18, its coal pier next to Cramp Shipyard, had a thawing shed to defrost simultaneously 55 carloads of frozen coal in winter. It could dump coal at the rate of 30 railcars per hour, and its yard permitted the handling of 771 railcars at a time. Other bulk cargo piers included Pier 14 for receiving ores and raw sugar for the nearby National Sugar refinery at the foot of Shackamaxon Street, and Pier E, completed in 1927. Pier E was used for exporting grain with an unloading capacity of 8,000 bushels per hour and was connected to a grain elevator with a 3.5 million-bushel capacity. The Philadelphia and Reading also maintained its own general cargo piers here, Piers A, B, C and D, as well as three others at the foot of Willow Street, Piers 24, 25 and 27 North. At Port Richmond's Pier G, the P&R boasted of having a derrick with 100 tons of lift capacity, the largest privately owned crane on the Atlantic coast. Fishtowners of a certain age can recall the pungent aroma of a trainload of gondolas loaded with raw sugarcane trundling down Penn Street from Pier 14 to the refinery, and the spectacular fire that consumed the Port Richmond general cargo piers A, C and D in October 1974, when the Philadelphia Fire Department had to recruit volunteers from the neighborhood to help with all its hoses.

The Pennsylvania Railroad focused its investments on bulk facilities in South Philadelphia, at Greenwich Point and Girard Point, and on general cargo facilities, Piers 55, 56 and 57, at the foot of Federal Street, site of the old Navy Yard that it had acquired after the Civil War. In 1881, its Girard Point Storage Company developed a grain elevator that was replaced by a much larger one at Pier 3 in 1914, and demolished in 2008. This grain elevator had an extensive system of supporting tracks in the appropriately named "Mud Yard" near the Schuylkill River, which also supported the PRR's ore pier, Pier 1. The development of Greenwich Point started with a PRR coal pier at the foot of Packer Avenue, but grew quickly after the removal of the two Delaware River islands caused filled land to be created where the League Island back channel had flowed. The growth of traffic below Washington Avenue coincided with the rapid development of this area of the city, and complaints grew about the PRR's trains, and to a lesser extent those of the B&O, blocking highway crossings. The problem on Washington Avenue was particularly severe, leading to calls for separation of the rail and street grades, with the railroad tracks to be elevated. The city and the two railroads negotiated the "South Philadelphia Agreement" in 1914, calling for tracks running north-south on the east bank of the Schuylkill River to be elevated, with the railroads sharing a common viaduct running above 25th Street, and for tracks crossing South Philadelphia from east to west to be shifted as far south as possible in order to avoid creating any more grade crossings. The plan for elevating the track on Washington Avenue was never implemented, and rail activity on that street finally terminated with the advent of Conrail. As an inducement for the railroads' cooperation, the city divided the new filled land of the back channel between them. This led to the PRR making major investments along their Delaware Extension, including the largest Philadelphia railyard, Greenwich. The B&O failed to develop their new property, and eventually sold it to the Navy for their Mustin Air Field.[1]

Along their Delaware Extension, the PRR constructed its produce terminal and refrigerated warehouse on the south side of Oregon Avenue, at Weccacoe Street, completed in 1928. It also built new coal unloading facilities at Pier 124, completed in 1929, and undertook an extensive expansion of the Greenwich railyard in 1944. Its final major investment there, Pier 122, was completed in 1954 to service ore ships bound up the Delaware River to the new US Steel Fairless Works in Bucks County, where the Delaware's shallower draft required certain ships to be lightered in Philadelphia before proceeding upriver.

The development of intermodal handling of general cargo in the 1950s had major impacts on the Port of Philadelphia. A story is told about the father of intermodal shipping, Malcom McLean, who in 1956 launched the concept by hauling truck trailers as deck cargo on two tankers, each with a capacity for 58 35-foot containers. McLean originally wanted to develop his "Sea-Land Services" intermodal facility at the Reading Railroad's Port Richmond Terminal, but was turned down and instead gravitated to New York. In 1956, the Port Authority of New York and New Jersey began development of a 700-acre containerport in the New Jersey Meadowlands, and the rest, as they say, is history. Whether the McLean story is true, the concept of intermodal truck-train shipping had been around since the 1920s, but had been held back by inflexible Interstate Commerce Commission regulations and had only received authorization in 1953, when the ICC issued a favorable ruling to the New Haven Rail Road, finding that through routes and joint rates between railroads and motor carriers were permissible.

▶ The Baltimore and Ohio Railroad's freight stations and team tracks in Philadelphia, 1926 (Illustration from *The Port of Philadelphia: Its History, Facilities and Advantages*, Department of Wharves, Docks and Ferries, 1926).

PHILADELPHIA, PENNA.

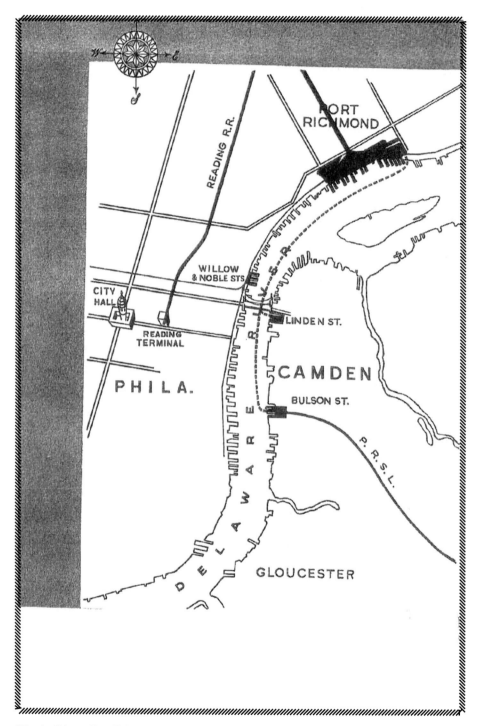

"The facilities at Port Richmond," an excerpt from a Reading Lines brochure of the 1950s (From the collection of John P. McGreevy).

the facilities at Port Richmond

Direct rail facilities for ship-side loading and unloading are not unusual, in port facilities, but rare indeed is the concentration of rail service that exists at Port Richmond. This tidewater terminal contains within its limits approximately 85 miles of railroad track with a yard storage capacity of 5,600 cars. This capacity provides for ready movement to or from the appropriate pier, and permits fast rail movement to or from any part of the country.

Later pages of this booklet present the facilities available at Port Richmond for handling various classes of cargo. Backing up all of these handling facilities is the convenience and speed of rail transportation facilitated by ample track capacity within the terminal area to assure rapid classification and delivery, or assembling and dispatching.

In addition, the Belt Line Railroad, operated along Philadelphia's entire water front, connects the Reading Lines with the Baltimore & Ohio and Pennsylvania Railroad Systems, making Port Richmond facilities readily available to all sections of the port.

A small section of the yard facilities at Port Richmond.

Philadelphia's early intermodal truck-rail terminals were located on the Reading at Wayne Junction and on the PRR at their Philadelphia and Trenton Railroad terminus at Kensington Avenue and Berks Streets. The B&O's terminal was at 24th and Jackson Streets. These facilities were quickly outgrown, and by 1976, they included: on the PRR (by then the Penn Central) at the Meadows Yard at Church Street and Aramingo Avenue in Bridesburg; at Erie Avenue Yard on the Reading, and at Snyder Avenue Yard on the B&O (by then the Chessie System) on the site of what had been their produce terminal on South Delaware Avenue. The Penn Central also had a Mail Van terminal in its 52nd Street railyard.[12]

The regional rail reorganization process, completed in April 1976 with the creation of Conrail, was followed in the early 1980s with a wave of deregulation that swept through all modes of freight transportation. With the deregulation of railroads and the trucking industry, companies no longer had to apply to the ICC for authorization to change routes or charges, but only to file tariffs. Traffic now flowed to those routes that were the most economical to operate. The final piece of deregulatory legislation was the Shipping Act of 1984, which accomplished the same outcome for ocean shipping. With the terminal location decisions of shipping lines no longer regulated, these lines developed fewer but larger terminals, called load centers, and this had a negative impact on smaller ports, or on ports whose hinterland connections were less direct. The Port of Philadelphia's Moyamensing and Southwark piers remained quite active because of their stevedores' expertise in handling cocoa beans and paper cargo that did not lend themselves to containerization. But the Philadelphia Port Corporation, the 1964 successor to the Department of Wharves, Docks and Ferries, struggled to maintain traffic at its two container facilities: Packer Avenue Marine Terminal, constructed on lands at Greenwich Point purchased from the PRR, and Tioga Marine Terminal, opened in October 1971 on a site adjacent to Port Richmond Terminal purchased from the Reading. That marketing effort became more difficult in the early 1980s when double-stack container trains made their debut in the Port of New York.

Among the various lines that Conrail inherited, one of them, the old Erie main line running across southern New York State (the "southern tier line"), had particularly good height clearances. It was discovered that stacking one container atop another was possible on this line if a relatively few height clearance obstructions could be eliminated. A train thus loaded could operate at double the capacity of a single-stack train, but with the same size of crew and only marginally more fuel consumption. Such trains could run as an economical land bridge between East and

▶ Philadelphia area railroad facilities (Philadelphia City Planning Commission map, January 1971). Like a calm before the storm, this map shows rail facilities shortly before the advent of Amtrak, the regional rail reorganization that created Conrail and led to Conrail's abandonment of underperforming branch lines and SEPTA's assumption of Conrail's commuter rail responsibilities.

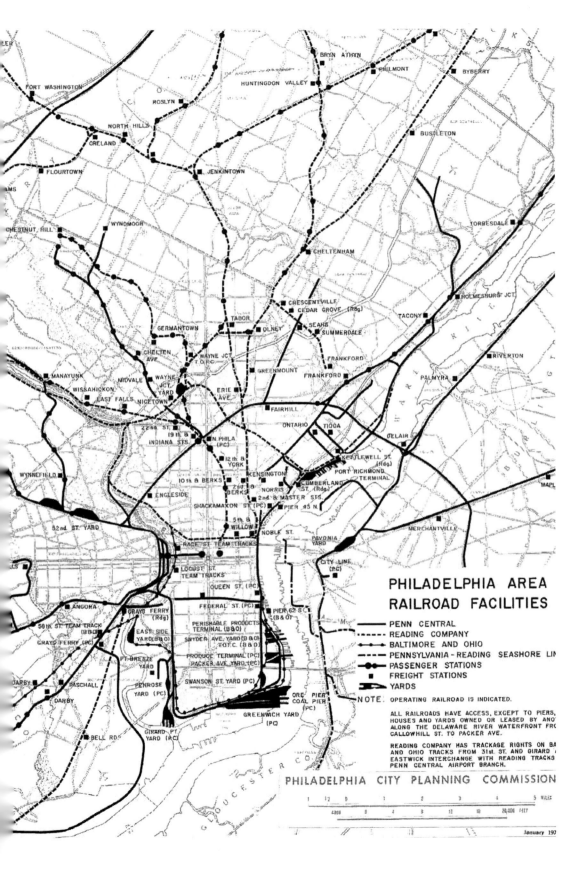

PHILADELPHIA AREA RAILROAD FACILITIES

PENN CENTRAL
------- READING COMPANY
•—•— BALTIMORE AND OHIO
—•—•— PENNSYLVANIA - READING SEASHORE LIN[E]
●—● PASSENGER STATIONS
■ FREIGHT STATIONS
▬ YARDS

NOTE: OPERATING RAILROAD IS INDICATED.

ALL RAILROADS HAVE ACCESS, EXCEPT TO PIERS,
HOUSES AND YARDS OWNED OR LEASED BY ANO[THER]
ALONG THE DELAWARE RIVER WATERFRONT FRO[M]
CALLOWHILL ST. TO PACKER AVE.

READING COMPANY HAS TRACKAGE RIGHTS ON BA[LTIMORE]
AND OHIO TRACKS FROM 31st. ST. AND GIRARD [AVE.]
EASTWICK INTERCHANGE WITH READING TRACKS
PENN CENTRAL AIRPORT BRANCH.

PHILADELPHIA CITY PLANNING COMMISSION

January 197[0]

The Reading's Port Richmond Terminal with Cramp Shipyard in the foreground (Courtesy of The Library Company of Philadelphia).

West Coasts. As a result, Asian container ships need not sail to North Atlantic ports, and European ships no longer needed to call on Pacific ports if they made use of this land bridge. The State of New York enthusiastically funded these clearance improvements. In contrast, the rail routes into Philadelphia passed through numerous tunnels and underpasses, and the effort to achieve double-stack capacity took two decades to complete here.

Conrail was naturally interested in maximizing utilization of its economical double-stack routes, and stymied with the intermodal terminals that it had inherited in Philadelphia, which were small and poorly situated relative to the routes with good height clearance. Early on, Conrail closed its Reading Erie Avenue and Penn Central Meadows terminals along with a Mail Van terminal at 52nd Street Yard in Philadelphia and consolidated them in Morrisville, an expensive truck haul from the Philadelphia Port Corporation's container terminals.

The "dray" to Morrisville in Bucks County was painful to the port, and two of its leading participants, Holt Cargo Systems and Barthco International, a "commercial house" or freight forwarder and custom house broker, pooled their resources. They established an intermodal yard on railroad tracks in the bed of Delaware Avenue near Packer Avenue Marine Terminal, operating with little more authorization than a temporary street closing permit from the Philadelphia Streets Department. Among their customers was Canadian Pacific Railroad, which had recently purchased the Delaware and Hudson. Their facility, known as "Ameriport," was later acquired by the Delaware River Port Authority and relocated onto land leased from Conrail at Greenwich Yard. Ameriport continued in operation until CSX created its own intermodal facility elsewhere on the Greenwich railyard property, providing the port with an economical alternative to Morrisville. CSX now provides the Canadian Pacific with intermodal terminal services at their new Greenwich terminal.

Chessie System, by now CSX Transportation, continued to handle container traffic through its Snyder Avenue terminal, thus providing Packer Marine Terminal with hinterland rail access. With new competitor Conrail replacing its old partner Reading, Chessie System now found its friendly gateway northward at Park Junction near Philadelphia's Art Museum to have become a chokepoint, the railroad equivalent of "Checkpoint Charlie," and its Philadelphia terminal facilities were now the northernmost on what had just become a stub-end system. Denied through routing northward, Chessie now launched an aggressive trucking operation that penetrated markets in New Jersey, New York and even into New England from its Snyder Avenue intermodal railyard, but its single-stack limitation was reflected in the quality of its services and rates. Delaware and Hudson Railroad, introduced into the Northeastern rail market by the regional rail reorganization with the U.S. Railway Association trying to maintain a fig leaf of east-west rail service competitive with Conrail, has been able to establish a toehold at the Philadelphia Navy Yard, where it operates a conventional railyard.

Conrail inherited two competing sets of waterfront terminals in Philadelphia, and not enough business to sustain even one of them. Port Richmond's coal pier (Pier 18) was kept in operation principally to ship anthracite to American military bases in Germany, even though there was adequate coal there to purchase for them, but this inefficient arrangement was driven by political considerations. The prime mover was the anthracite region's theatrical congressman, Dan Flood—a dapper, white-suited character with a waxed moustache who preferred dressing in top hat, tails and cane, and who recited Shakespeare during election rallies. But Flood protected the anthracite industry, at least until he resigned from Congress in 1980 after being censured for bribery. The congressman's departure marked the end of anthracite shipping at Port Richmond.

Performing investment triage with its limited resources, Conrail built up Greenwich but starved Port Richmond. The American steam coal industry took on new overseas customers in the wake of the petroleum shocks of the 1970s, and

Conrail borrowed $40 million from the Commonwealth of Pennsylvania to overhaul its Greenwich coal pier (Pier 124). A private investor, Elias Kulukundis, attempted to revive coal exports at Port Richmond, but to no avail. Alas, neither Pier 124 nor Port Richmond Terminal provided for ground storage of coal, instead keeping the coal in the railcars awaiting the ship. This was a poor use of railroad equipment as the ship's arrival could vary considerably from its schedule. It was not a problem at Maryland and Virginia coal terminals where ground storage was available, and by the 1990s, Conrail had also shut down Pier 124. The ore import business declined as Pennsylvania mills ceased production in the 1970s, and Conrail, having abandoned its Port Richmond ore pier (Pier 14), finally closed Pier 122, its Greenwich ore operation, and sold it to the Philadelphia Regional Port Authority, owner of the adjacent Packer Avenue Marine (container) Terminal.

Conrail also inherited two sets of grain terminals, the Reading's Pier E at Port Richmond and the Penn Central's Pier 3 at Girard Point. While the completion of the Saint Lawrence Seaway in 1958 diverted much of the Midwest's grain exports away from Atlantic ports, Pier 3 remained competitive into the early 1980s, particularly during the months when the seaway was frozen. At Pier 3, Roger Larkin's successful Tidewater Grain Company did not survive his death, and at Pier E, Bunge Corporation ceased operations in 1976 after renovating the grain elevator. Conrail demolished the Port Richmond grain elevator in 1999. Pier 3 was eventually sold and its grain elevator demolished in 2008.

In 1996, Conrail and CSX announced what they termed a merger of equals, but this brought immediate negative reaction from shippers' organizations, port authorities and most ominously from Norfolk Southern, which promptly launched a hostile takeover bid. A compromise was reached the following year with CSX and Norfolk Southern agreeing to jointly buy out Conrail, with NS acquiring 58 percent of its assets, including 6,000 route miles, and CSX claiming 42 percent of Conrail's assets, with 3,600 route miles. Norfolk Southern's acquisitions generally were lines that had been part of its former parent, the Pennsylvania Railroad, as "the child became the father of the man," while CSX claimed the vestiges of the New York Central. J.P. Morgan would have been pleased. In three markets where Conrail assets were too intermingled to separate either logically or economically between the buyers, an entity known as Conrail Shared Assets Organization (CSAO) was created to allow CSX and NS to jointly manage operations in these markets— Philadelphia, Northern New Jersey and Detroit. After approval by the federal Surface Transportation Board in June 1998, reorganized operations began, albeit with a rocky start, as information technology incompatibilities hamstrung cargo as well as data routings, particularly on Norfolk Southern, until finally resolved nine months later.

The sale of Conrail to CSX and Norfolk Southern has had mixed impacts on Philadelphia. On the one hand, the headquarters functions that employed thousands in the city have now all but disappeared. Conrail's office tower, constructed in the late 1980s at 20th and Market Streets, is now mostly empty of railroad employees. The PRR's West Philadelphia Office Building now houses condominiums where clerks once toiled over waybills. CSAO has few employees based in Philadelphia, with most working in Mount Laurel, New Jersey. Little more than track and structures remain of the once-mighty Reading and Pennsylvania Railroad presence in Philadelphia. Conrail, perhaps unknowingly taking its cue from Steven Girard, was a major donor to civic causes in Philadelphia, a benefactor of many charities, and it is questionable whether current railroad industry beneficence approaches what Conrail had given.

On the other hand, CSX has made the investments necessary to bring the port and the city into the modern transportation age, constructing a state-of-the-art intermodal facility with double-stack capability at the old PRR Greenwich yard, and improving height clearances (with generous funding from the Commonwealth of Pennsylvania) so that the port can be competitive again. CSX's Greenwich investments have been particularly beneficial to Packer Avenue Marine Terminal, for which major expansion is planned by its owner, the Philadelphia Regional Port Authority, a state agency. CSX has sold Greenwich Pier 124 to the PRPA, along with adjacent acreage, to permit substantial expansion of the adjacent PRPA container terminal.

One of the most perplexing questions facing CSX after it acquired its portion of Conrail was what to do with Philadelphia. Was Philadelphia the end of the old Baltimore and Ohio route through Maryland, or the end of the New York Central/Reading route through New Jersey? The "B&O route" was John W. Garrett's creation, discussed in Chapter 3, and the "NYC route" was a legacy of Franklin Gowen's efforts to patch together a route to New York Harbor using the P&R, North Penn, and Delaware and Bound Brook Railroads, and his friend William Vanderbilt's Jersey Central route, discussed in Chapter 4. Neither the B&O nor the NYC route was double-stack-cleared in 1998. Running west on the B&O required first going all the way south to Washington, D.C. via Baltimore, but running on the NYC route actually required going initially east in order to move west. There was no history of serving Philadelphia over the NYC route because Conrail and its predecessors had serviced the city's east-west traffic via the PRR and Reading routes, which were not designated to CSX in the Conrail sale.

The CSX decision was influenced by the character of the routes. The Baltimore and Ohio is a coal and merchandise railroad. The New York Central is a passenger railroad adapted to higher-speed intermodal and automotive traffic. Philadelphia's CSX intermodal service was ultimately designed onto the NYC network as something new. The decision to end the last pair of Philadelphia east-west intermodal trains over the old B&O was an emotional and agonizing one.

With this new routing pattern, CSX also overcame the disadvantage of Philadelphia routes not having enough traffic volume to sustain more frequent service. By routing its intermodal trains over the Port of New York's main route, Philadelphia shippers could now capitalize on New York's superior service frequency. This special advantage is worth further exploiting as part of Philadelphia's marketing and economic development efforts.

Norfolk Southern's involvement in improving Philadelphia logistics is less clear. In the negotiations leading up to the approval of the Conrail sale, NS had offered to build a $16 million intermodal terminal on the grounds of the former Philadelphia Navy Base, and in fact completed construction, but the facility has never opened. In November 2009, an announcement was made that Norfolk Southern would expand this facility at a cost of $11 million, with $5 million to be provided by the Commonwealth of Pennsylvania, as part of Norfolk's multi-state intermodal upgrade of its Crescent Corridor, with construction starting in mid-2010. As of mid-2011, the writer was informed that the Commonwealth had redirected its Navy Yard contribution, at the railroad's request, to another NS project at Harrisburg. Norfolk Southern's facility investment decisions in Philadelphia are puzzling, to say the least, and in the Philadelphia region, NS appears to be a junior partner with CSX in managing and using their shared Conrail assets, in marked contrast to Norfolk's aggressive, competitive stance in other markets.

One rail intermodal chokepoint that remains to be addressed is rail access to Tioga Marine Terminal. The double-stacked line at Nicetown near this terminal connects to the final, two-mile segment of Moncure Robinson's original Port Richmond Branch, whose height clearance is woefully inadequate. This branch, essentially a series of railroad underpasses with city streets above it for a distance of two miles back to Nicetown, could handle significantly higher freight volumes for the Philadelphia waterfront. This is traffic identified by Tioga's terminal operator Bob Palaima, president of Delaware River Stevedores, that could be handled competitively there, but now must be turned away because of this branch's height clearance limitation. The branch is treated as an orphan by Conrail Shared Assets, Norfolk Southern and CSX. It really needs a guardian.

The Philadelphia shipbuilding industry, dying with Cramp Shipyard in 1945, has been resurrected at the Philadelphia Navy Base by Aker, utilizing the enormous dry docks abandoned when the Navy departed, and enormous public subsidies. Alas, there is no happy ending to Philadelphia's steel industry. Midvale Steel Company, acquired by Heppenstall Steel in 1955, remained in operation servicing its primary customer base—the Defense Department, the power generation industry and Budd—into the 1970s. At Budd's urging, the mill had uniquely large electric arc ovens whose dimensions allowed Midvale to produce oversized forgings, including the nickel rings used to isolate radioactive material on atomic submarines and the rotors needed in power plants. The single forging of the nickel rings eliminated the need for welds, which had been shown to leak radiation. The mill had a separate building, owned by the Defense Industrial Reserve, where barrels for the Army's 175-millimeter howitzers were produced. Midvale continued to be a specialty steel mill, not a volume one.

In the mid-1970s, Midvale Heppenstall Steel Company faced an especially serious labor-management impasse. Midvale paid its workers less than other steel mills and enjoyed greater flexibility in its work rules, a legacy of the Taylor era. After Midvale merged its operations with Heppenstall Steel Company's Pittsburgh plant, the Midvale steelworkers' union demanded contract parity with the Pittsburgh mill, but management believed that its business could not sustain such an increase in its labor expense and remain profitable. In desperation, Midvale's officers called on the City of Philadelphia to step into the negotiations, and the city's Commerce Department director, Harry Bellinger, dispatched City Economist Jan Vagassky to try to find an acceptable alternative. Midvale's chief operating officer, Paul North, provided Vagassky with the company's financial data, and Vagassky became convinced that granting parity would bankrupt the company. He explained this finding to the union's officials, but was told that their dignity was offended by not having the same contract as their Pittsburgh counterparts. Seeking some other solution and cognizant of Midvale's role in national defense, Vagassky and North contacted the local congressman, Robert N.C. Nix Sr., and requested a meeting, which was held in Washington. They were ushered into his office by his aides and introduced to him. Nix sat at his desk, wearing opaque sunglasses, his chin propped in his palm, elbow on the table, and seemed not to acknowledge his visitors or speak during the meeting. His complexion was ashen, and he appeared unwell. Afterward, North and Vagassky were left to wonder whether Congressman Nix had even been conscious during their time with him. Nothing resulted from the meeting. Midvale proved to be a harbinger for the Pennsylvania steel industry's impending collapse, brought on by the same issues of compensation and work rules.

Midvale Heppenstall declared bankruptcy and closed. But the company owned a critical new technology known as "core remelt" that allowed the cooling of oversized forgings slowly and evenly, ensuring consistent hardness throughout the finished product, and avoiding rejections and rework that often resulted from inadequate cooling. This technology was of particular value to the power generation industry, whose large rotors would shatter if not cooled properly. A British entrepreneur, Ian Westwood-Booth, attempted to revive Midvale in order to capitalize on this core remelt technology, but investment was not forthcoming. The plant eventually was sold, its equipment auctioned off, its patent rights sold, and its buildings either demolished or reused by other businesses. Midvale joined Baldwin and Cramp, the Penn Central and Reading, Budd, John Evans' Sons and the renamed Delaware Avenue—Philadelphia institutions existing only in memory.

References

1. Department of Wharves, Docks and Ferries, *The Port of Philadelphia: Its History, Facilities and Advantages* (Philadelphia: DWDF, 1926), gives an account of the beginnings of the port and Delaware Avenue, reminiscences of the port in the 19th century by surviving port wardens, and the pier construction program of 1907 to 1926.
2. Rudolph J. Walther, *Happenings in Ye Olde Philadelphia, 1690–1900* (Philadelphia: Walther Printing House, 1925), includes descriptions of life in Camptown-Fishtown, the Philadelphia Fish Market, and the shipbuilding and fishing industries.
3. David Burlong Tyler, *The Bay and River Delaware* (Cambridge, MD: Cornell Maritime Press, 1955), discusses the shipbuilding industry on the Delaware and Christiana Rivers.
4. Peter Binzen, "Cradle of American shipbuilding" (*The Philadelphia Inquirer,* November 3, 1997), gives a history of Philadelphia's shipbuilding industry and includes a quotation by Charles Cramp.
5. Lini S. Kadaba, "A sunken ship, a rising peace" (*The Philadelphia Inquirer,* February 10, 1992), deals with the ceremony honoring the 88th anniversary of the sinking of the Russian battleship *Variag.*
6. John D. Alden, *The American Steel Navy* (Annapolis, MD: Naval Institute Press; New York, American Heritage Press, 1972), discusses the construction of the "ABCD ships" and others from 1883 to1909, as well as attitudes of U.S. Presidents toward War Department shipbuilding contracts.
7. Jay V. Hare, *History of the Reading* (serialized in *The Pilot* and *Philadelphia and Reading Railroad Men,* May 1909 to February 1914), later published in book form (Philadelphia: John Henry Strock, 1966), gives an account of the purchase, design, construction and operation of Port Richmond Terminal.
8. George H. Burgess and Miles C. Kennedy, *Centennial History of the Pennsylvania Railroad* (Philadelphia: The Pennsylvania Railroad, 1949), discusses the PRR's expansion onto the Philadelphia waterfront, the purchase of Cramp steamships, the development of piers and shipping terminals, the American Steamship Line, and the Produce and Refrigerated Terminal.
9. *The Midvale Century* (Philadelphia: Midvale-Heppenstall Steel Company, 1967) gives a full account of the history of the Midvale Steel Company and the Edward G. Budd Company.
10. James J.D. Lynch, Jr., *The Chestnut Hill and Fort Washington Branches* (Philadelphia: Philadelphia Chapter, PRR Technical and Historical Society, 1982), discusses the Midvale Branch and the Edward G. Budd Company.
11. *Encyclopedia Americana* (1955 Edition) gives a good history of steelmaking, welding and stamping in the United States.